RISE

RISE

MARK BOURIS

hachette
AUSTRALIA

hachette
AUSTRALIA

Published in Australia and New Zealand in 2021
by Hachette Australia
(an imprint of Hachette Australia Pty Limited)
Level 17, 207 Kent Street, Sydney NSW 2000
www.hachette.com.au

10 9 8 7 6 5 4 3 2 1

A catalogue record for this
book is available from the
National Library of Australia

ISBN: 978 0 7336 4573 0 (paperback)

Cover design by Christabella Designs
Cover image courtesy of Mark Bouris
Typeset in Sabon LT Std by Kirby Jones
Printed and bound in Great Britain by Clays Ltd, Elcograf S.p.A.

The paper this book is printed on is certified against the Forest Stewardship Council® Standards. McPherson's Printing Group holds FSC® chain of custody certification SA-COC-005379. FSC® promotes environmentally responsible, socially beneficial and economically viable management of the world's forests.

To all the ambitious, the early risers,
the hard workers, the hustlers and the big thinkers.
This book is for you.

CONTENTS

A Note About You

They say a crisis reveals your true character. If that's the case, then we should be bloody proud.

Maybe you've heard me talk about it before, but it needs repeating. Australian small business owners are tough. Like our land, you're resilient, possessing an inner strength that you don't even know you have until the hard times come along.

It still gives me goosebumps when I reflect on your attitude to the shocks you've faced in the last year. Devastating bushfires, storms, floods and a pandemic. The hits kept coming. It's not been easy and, unfortunately, I know not every business will make it through these recent times. No matter what, though, you can be seriously proud of the grit and resolve that you've already demonstrated.

In all aspects of life, it is when you are knocked down that your true colours are revealed. I know many of you will use adversity to drive yourselves to a different path to success. In *Rise*, I want to be in your corner, helping you harness disruption and focus your strengths so you can succeed in business and in life no matter what comes at you.

Mark Bouris

Introduction

Let's start with what should already be obvious; if you know me, you'll know that this isn't just another one of those boring self-help books you've read a thousand times before. You know, the ones where you get through a chapter, maybe even two, of gentle reassurances and overused clichés before it's abandoned to gather dust on your bookshelf, or in the bin – which is exactly where most of them belong.

That's just not my style. I don't bullshit anyone, and I don't waste time – least of all my own. So, let's be honest with each other. You don't think you can do it, do you? You think you and I are somehow different? That's absolute nonsense.

Some people I know see me getting really energised, and they look at me – and how old I am – and they think,

How does he do it? And people I don't know, but who've read about me, see me as having done something successful and they ask the same question. Because everybody wants the 'how to' handbook. I also think people see me as an open person, I pretty much say what I think. I won't keep any secrets. I'll tell everybody what I know if they ask me. That's what this book's about. Sharing what I know about business, about life and about succeeding.

I grew up in Punchbowl, which back then was the very heart of Sydney's working-class western suburbs. My father worked his arse off in a nearby factory, and when he finally knocked off for the day he then picked up yet more work. But spare money was never a part of our lives. Born with a silver spoon? There were some nights we were lucky to even have a spoon at all.

But I recognised something early on that you need to recognise, too. That I would have to be my best, and often only, asset. My energy, my drive, my willingness to work my arse off – all of that was more valuable to me than any amount of money. It's what separated me from the pack, and what will separate you from it as well. There are no easy rides, but if you put smart effort in, good things can happen for you.

You might be sitting there thinking, *I can't do that, I can't do what he does, I can't be a Mark Bouris.* But the fact is, you can. Anyone can. And I'm going to show you how. In this book I'll tell you my story and punctuate that tale with concentrated ideas that are lessons to help you. This is from my experience, from what I've encountered; there will be a little of what I think, maybe too much in some chapters, but most of the information on these pages is drawn from what I did, what I do, what I read, what I watch and who I've worked with. It's what I've learned.

A lot of the focus in this book is about entrepreneurs and small business owners, the sole traders and the self-employed, but the advice is relevant to anyone who wants to make change in their working life. If you've ever thought about striking out on your own, then this is a must-read book for you. And when I speak of entrepreneurs it doesn't mean finance gurus or tech giants, it means any innovator creating a new business.

My advice won't always be nice, and it won't always be friendly, but it will be the cold, hard truth, no matter what. Because it's time to cut the bullshit and get down to business.

up a business. He soon bought the downstairs floor, then he bought the middle floor, then the next floor. In the end, he owned the whole building in George Street. In those days, that meant he was pretty wealthy. He had two houses in Maroubra as well. Things were looking good for the family and that move from Greece was seen as a wise one. But then my dad fell in love with my mum, Marsha (and unfortunately, she wasn't Greek). That was enough for my dad to be left out of his father's will so he didn't inherit any of my grandfather's wealth.

My mum was of Irish background, she was a strong person, very smart and intellectually sophisticated. She was very beautiful too – quite stunning. She didn't have a formal education but she read a lot. She came from a musical family, whereas Dad had come from an agrarian family. All her siblings were sisters; Dad had come from a family of all brothers. They had very different backgrounds.

Mum and Dad moved to Punchbowl – the first people to settle in the newly built street – and I was born in 1956. I can't say that I had a particularly tough upbringing. We didn't have a lot of money, but we weren't church-mouse poor either. There were difficult times though. When the economy slowed and Australia hit a recession in 1961, my dad lost his factory job, just like everyone else. Every time there was a recession, my dad would lose his job because the factories would close down. In Australia we've hit several serious speedbumps: 1961, 1971, 1977, 1981 and now 2020. But manufacturing has faced challenges even when the country has not been in recession, and factory workers know what I am talking about. Luckily, even when Dad was out of work, my family were looked after. The butcher used to put meat on our doorstep on Saturday afternoon – whatever he had that he didn't sell and couldn't keep for the next week. I never, ever thought to myself, *Ah, wow, these are really hard times*, it didn't really enter my mind at all.

Dad worked in the factory behind where we lived. For half of his full-time working life he worked in that factory, and the other half of his life he worked in another factory. He wasn't shy of hard work. He worked long hours, supplementing the factory incomes with a lot of extra jobs whenever and wherever he could.

Dad was never really educated. He went to school for one year in Australia and then, initially, worked in his dad's business. All his brothers did too. That was the Greek tradition. It was just, 'Stuff school, you're coming to work for me.' In the café you waited or you cooked or you'd do something else. No slackers allowed. In return for working for his dad my father got to live at home with all his brothers, all lined up in a row. All six boys sleeping in one room. Six beds. All in one room.

Mum was working in those days at Farmers (Farmer and Company), which became a part of Grace Bros. and is now Myer. She needed more money because she was also raising her two sisters on her own. Her sisters grew up with us and lived with my family. Two of my dad's brothers lived with us as well. So, in our house there were two of Mum's sisters, two of Dad's brothers, plus me, my brother and sister, and Mum and Dad. It was only a three-bedroom house. I don't know how we managed it. I honestly can't remember where everyone slept. We somehow fitted in between each other. I do remember I shared a room with my brother. He and I slept in one room and everyone else occupied the other rooms. When people ask if I was bred tough – well, it depends what you mean by that. I grew up knowing you had to work to earn money and that money was for looking after your family.

> 'There is definitely a "hardworking"
> gene in my family's DNA.'

Growing up watching how my mum and dad lived means the concept of hard work is important to me. It is actually an ethic that helps define what I am about. And more importantly, I think it's a cornerstone to create a solid foundation of any business. If you want to change your life, build your business and chase your goals but you aren't prepared to put everything you have into achieving that, then put this book down now.

Hard work is important

You're the only one who can make a change in your life. Forget about others telling you about success, because your success will be different from anyone else's. Forget about secret methods of success; forget about getting caught up in social media feeds – focus on you. Work hard and relentlessly back yourself. Because at the end of the day, everything is on you.

•

I may not have been born with that silver spoon everyone raves about, but I inherited something more important to long-term success: a strong model of what a work ethic looks like.

I never felt like I missed out on anything as I grew older, but I was acutely aware of not having a lot of money to waste. My dad would get me a bike for Christmas, but it would be a second-hand bike, and he would have repainted it. Other kids in the street would get a brand-new bike. It didn't bother me, but I was aware of it.

My mother made me pursue music outside of school. It was something she aspired for us to do because her father was a musician, a lot of people in her family were musicians. I had piano lessons and I knew that was a privilege. My parents had to work hard to make the extra money for the music lessons for me and my brother. They bought a piano and I knew that was a big deal. I knew they had to work extra hard to get that for us.

Mum also got us into swimming. My mum couldn't swim, my dad couldn't swim. My dad never saw the sea until he got onto the ship to come to Australia. He'd never had fish. He hadn't had running water in his home in Greece. They didn't have a toilet. They had to get the water from a well. Swimming was the last thing on his mind.

When I was very young at school we had a swimming carnival at Bankstown Olympic Swimming Pool. One year, when the races were on, I don't know what possessed me, but next thing I remember I was on the blocks ready to jump. I couldn't swim. On the starter's orders I jumped off and I dog-paddled for fifty metres. It was like running a hundred kilometres. I struggled and I came last. It didn't bother me too much, but my mother said, 'That's never going to happen again.' So she went and got me some swimming lessons. After I made it through swimming lessons, she got me into a swim squad and then, next thing you know, the following year, I won the school's swim event for my age group. I won it.

Mum, she was a strong personality. She was purposeful in everything she did and Dad always supported her in every way he could. Whether it was working hard and paying the bills, or getting up at midnight to go on a milk run and coming home at six in the morning, and then going into the factory at 7 am – that's what he would do.

For a long time he worked two jobs, from midnight through to four o'clock the next day, just to make sure that the few extra bob that he'd get would allow me my piano and swimming lessons. That was because Mum would have said to him, 'We don't want our son to be coming last.'

Mum often talked about why she'd made those choices. She used to tell me that it broke her heart to see her son come last. As I said, it didn't bother me, I didn't think about it because I was only seven or eight, but it broke her heart to see her son struggle.

My Irish Catholic mum didn't have such a great upbringing. She loved her father. They were really close. But she never talked about her mother. She was a drunk and she'd left my mother's father and remarried another guy. I never met my grandfather on my mum's side either. He was an alcoholic too, and a gambler. All of this drunkenness was the reason my mother's two younger sisters ended up moving in with us so my mother could look after them.

Mum never touched alcohol. She wouldn't drink. She wanted to be better than her parents were. She didn't want to be going through life dragging her arse along behind her because she was too drunk to look forward. She had much more potential. She was very bright but never had the opportunity to learn to play music, like I did. She'd had no support growing up, whereas my father had tremendous support from his brothers. All of the five boys were very close to each other and to their mother and father – they were a good family.

I lived with my grandmother on Dad's side when my grandfather passed away, a little later, when I was at university. She was a tiny old Greek lady and could only speak a few words of English. She had phrases like, 'You know, you know, you know' or 'Okay'. But she still couldn't say 'It is' – she used to say it in Greek.

Both Mum's and Dad's families had big influences on me. My dad's family were all really hardworking farmers, very rural, and they brought that with them to Australia.

The fact that every one of them worked relentlessly rubbed off on me. My mother's influence was more at an intellectual level: to be curious and be prepared to look at, and explore, other things. Although I didn't know it at the time, it would help me become the businessman I turned out to be.

Do not be intimidated

No one else at my school learned to play the piano. They all played football. Rugby league. Footy was why I eventually gave up the piano. I always wanted to be a football player. That's all I was interested in.

No one in my family knew anything about rugby league. My mum was from a family of all girls. Dad, being Greek, only knew about soccer. We didn't have television back in those days, it was all radio, so no one had seen people playing league.

When I was eight, in fourth class, I was at St John's school in Lakemba, where they played league. I came home one day and said I wanted to play footy with my mate, who I'd met at school. Mum said, 'I don't want you playing that.' Dad was more, 'Whatever.' He didn't even know the game. Mum relented, saying, 'Okay you can go and try out.' So, I went and tried out and I got in the side.

I ended up playing football for the school, and I became captain of the team. It was a pretty rough environment, the Canterbury–Bankstown district. We were the Catholic team full of Greeks, Italians and Lebanese and we played all the Aussie schools like Revesby and Greenacre. That's all changed now, culturally, in those areas. But back then, they were the white Aussie guys and we were the wogs or wops. Every week was a problem.

It was a different game then. In those days, parents on the sideline used to come onto the field and whack us. When we got in a brawl on the field, a lot of times the parents would be in a brawl on the sidelines as well. We would be fighting parents and parents would be fighting each other. It was that bad. Or referees would get clocked in the game. And I'm talking about games with thirteen-, fourteen-year-old boys.

My sons have experienced a bit of that, but what I went through was probably ten times as bad. And it was on all the time, at every game. Every single week. We used to cop shit from every other team, but it didn't get under my skin. It was what I grew up with and learned to accept. I think you accept whatever your 'normal' is, maybe because you have no relative measure of what's different. It didn't upset me, but maybe it made me more resilient because resilience is a comparative word relative to other

17

things, other people. Since I grew up in that environment, I wasn't intimidated by anything or anyone.

My dad knew nothing about representative footy. He didn't understand it at all. He didn't even know it existed, whereas all the other kids' parents knew about it and encouraged the boys to get into rep footy because they knew it was in first grade and you could get paid. It was a job and if you played for Canterbury–Bankstown – they were called the Berries in those days – you would, generally speaking, get picked up by somebody and get paid a sponsorship. Then you worked for them as well. You got a job. It was a way to guarantee employment. My dad didn't know any of this and my mum definitely knew less because, in the later years, she wouldn't even come to the games. Consequently, I had no idea either. No one ever discussed it with me.

One day a whole lot of kids on my team got invited to go and try out for Canterbury–Bankstown. I don't know whether I got asked or not. I knew nothing about it. My best friend told me he was going and I asked, 'What is it?' and he explained what it meant. I said, 'Oh wow. I didn't get asked for that, maybe I'm not good enough?' I remember telling my parents and it didn't really register with them but then the manager of the side said to me, 'Look, I'm going to get you a chance to try out for it, you go to Belmore Oval on such and such a night.' Night training was a big deal. I went down to Belmore Oval, put my boots on, did a training session, and then I met the coach at the club. He had played for the Canterbury–Bankstown team. There was an elimination process. It went on for four or five weeks and they had to pick twenty kids. I got picked as number nineteen. Given that league is thirteen players a team, it didn't register that number nineteen meant I was on the bench, not the run-on squad. I was just glad to have a Canterbury–Bankstown jersey with any number. I have a photograph of it.

I was happy. I'd train but didn't play. I'd sit on the bench. There were a few trial matches against St George and various other clubs and I sat on the bench for all of them. Then in the first game of the proper rep competition, one of the kids in the position that I was playing got injured. I'm on the bench and I hear, 'Bouris, you're on.' So, I ran on, number nineteen, and I thought, *I'm going to play really hard. I'm going to play my hardest.* I thought I was going okay until a punt hit me in the chest. Afterwards, the coach said, 'You played a good game. Well done.'

The next week I was on the bench again, but this time they put me on at half-time. The next game, I was in the run-on side and then I played the whole season. After the grand final against Manly, the coach from the other team brought in the football, the game ball, signed by all the other team members and presented it to me. I had no idea why as I wasn't the captain. I had no understanding of what it meant. I do today and I still have that football, or at least my dad does. We went to the awards night and I won Best and Fairest for the competition. I wasn't particularly talented, nor fast; I was pretty strong, relatively speaking, but mostly I was just willing.

•

'You don't wake up at eighteen and start an amazing business. It takes a long, long time and there's lots of building blocks in between.'

I wrote this recently and I'm reminded of it when I think about those early schoolboy football experiences. No matter how old you are no one is ever fully formed, I know I'm definitely not. We simply have to learn from failure and from experience, and the businesses we start and the things we do in our younger years will never match the complexity and sophistication of what we do later in our lives.

That's not to say that young people don't know what they're doing or that we shouldn't encourage young entrepreneurs to take a chance, but we need to acknowledge the long, hard slog of starting a business. Especially in an era when we all crave instant gratification. We need to acknowledge the uncomfortable mistakes we'll all no doubt make. Because when you're not uncomfortable, you're not growing. That growth can come even when you're sitting on the bench, waiting for your moment. But you've gotta wait and be patient.

•

The guys we played against at those levels of rep footy were all rough bastards. We were playing against Balmain, against Western Suburbs. And all the other clubs were trying to intimidate us. I wasn't prepared to be intimidated. I'd fight anybody. Literally fight. The rest of my team was much more talented than me – they could run fast and kick and all that sort of stuff – but I was willing to fight. I still am. I box and fight every year. I don't know what that's about. I just have that in me. It's always been there. Always. I actually enjoy it. When I was at school, I wouldn't pick a fight. Never. But if someone wanted to fight me, I'd fight him. No problem. Even today I'll box anyone. I've fought and sparred with all sorts of boxers including world champions like Danny Green, Jeff Fenech, Garth Wood.

'I'll never say no to fighting. It sounds bad but
it came in useful when I took on the banks at
Wizard – that willingness to take on anybody.'

This willingness did get me into trouble in my later teens a little bit, because I'd go out and have a few drinks, someone would say something and it'd be on. Sometimes the cops got involved and I'd get in trouble, but never anything really serious.

Somebody wrote an article on me many, many years ago in *The Australian*. It was the first article written about me when I'd just started Wizard. The journalist asked a mate of mine who I'd played football with, a friend who's known me my whole life, 'What was Mark like as a sportsman?' My mate's words were, 'Mark was probably a better fighter than he was a footballer.' I don't think he meant that I was necessarily a better boxer, but better at the fight than he was in terms of the game and where our abilities lay.

'Sometimes being better at the fight is
more important than being talented.'

Back in my rep football days, I believed in playing for my team. I still do. I believed in trying to win for my team and still do. I believed in not letting anybody intimidate us. Some of the opposition kids at fifteen, sixteen, had tattoos. Some of them already had the makings of beards at fifteen, which was intimidating, and sometimes they were bigger than us. Some of them looked like men and they may have looked older and tougher but I never shied away from the fight.

I think back to that period of my life and how I inherited my mother's intellectual willingness and my father's physical willingness. I think they're the two things I derived from both of them. Those two attributes have led me down two different paths over the years, business and boxing. Both require a willingness to fight. Boxing is one way I can express that combativeness, but I can express it through business too.

Cutting and sewing

I have a younger brother, Adrian, who's very different from me. Adrian's a very detailed person and I'm not. When he was a little kid, he would sit with Lego for five or six hours building. I couldn't be bothered. There was too much detail involved. Whereas Adrian is really brilliant with that stuff. Every deal I've ever done, whether with Kerry Packer, General Electric or Yellow Brick Road, my brother does the back end for me. We've worked on every deal together. We have an old saying, 'Mark cuts, Adrian sews.'

While detail might not be my thing, one skill I was gifted with is that I have good instincts. I've got good instincts about people and markets. Generally speaking, my instincts have been right. I went through a period of my life where I just acted on instincts and I was very successful, then I built this skill of being much more analytical and I went through a period where I was purely analytical, always over-analysing, and I missed things – I became paralysed with analysis. Now I use both these skills: my instincts and my ability to analyse.

What should you do if you're a businessperson who has good analytical skills but doesn't have good instincts? I think you're better off working with somebody else, not working for yourself.

Cut and sew. The person who works on their instincts is the person who cuts. If I make you a suit I have to be a really good cutter. I have to cut efficiently, leaving enough room to make mistakes, but that's not the suit. The suit's next stage is sewing. The person who sews needs to be precise. To make a beautiful suit you need a good fabric, a brilliant cutter and a great sewer. For me, the cutting is instinct, sewing is the analytical skill.

When I'm looking for people to come into my business, I sometimes need a cutter and sometimes I need a sewer. The cutter is more creative, they build big businesses. The sewer keeps it together. Often I'd rather cut my own stuff, but I do need sewers and my brother's the best sewer I've ever known. I'll conceive the deal, think about the deal, organise the deal and make the deal, but my brother stitches it up tight.

My brother's a tough son of a bitch. Kerry Packer tried to employ him three times to be his in-house counsel. My brother just told him to get stuffed. Told him, 'No, no. You can't have me no matter what amount of money you offer me, Kerry, I will never work for you.' Believe me, no one said that to Kerry Packer. Kerry was dealing with my brother through me. He couldn't believe it. He just kept upping the amount, 'I'll give him two million a year. I'll give him three million a year.' Adrian just kept responding with, 'Tell him I'm not interested.'

He was like this when we were kids. Always. Straight, solid. But he's like that with everything. In business, there's no off switch. It's just, 'We're going to do it. We're going to do it my way, every little detail is going to be one hundred per cent correct.' When he negotiates for me, I'll go and do the deal. He'll make it happen. He will never let one point pass. It doesn't matter if it's worth a dollar or a hundred million dollars. He will pursue one dollar as hard as he pursues the bigger number. I have to walk in and say, 'We're not going to worry about that one. Let's just worry about the hundred-million-dollar deals.' It just works. I am blessed with my brother.

•

I also have a younger sister, Jane. She's tough. She's lovely, but she's really tough on Adrian and me. Extraordinarily tough. Intellectually, physically – in every sense.

My sister doesn't work in the business. She works at Russell Investments, one of the big funds. She works full-time. She runs a house. She's been doing all this her whole life. Family, full-time work, looking out for Mum and Dad when Mum had motor neurone disease (MND). Looking out for my dad when Mum passed away.

My sister can do a thousand things at once and do them all precisely. She's a phenomenon when it comes to capability. It's ridiculous.

My dad is in his mid-eighties now, but he still climbs up on the roof. He's so independent. He paints the house, does the cleaning, does the washing and ironing every week, cooks for himself. He does everything. I go there every second Sunday. He looks really good. He's strong. He's fit, he's slim. He's not obsessed about it, but he's just naturally that way. Dad's really quite blessed in that regard.

•

Off the football field, I was generally a good student. Not always. I wasn't particularly interested in schoolwork, I wanted to play footy instead. But back when you did what was called the intermediate, which is Year 10 today, fourth year in my time, you had to do a set of exams. I got six A's. Maths and Science were my favourites, but I did Latin, French and Music.

I've got a good memory, especially for numbers. I was able to remember exactly which page something was written on. I knew if I read the book and read through the six or eight necessary chapters three times, I would remember everything when asked a question. I would be able to see where the answer to that question was sitting on the page.

As far as career ambitions went, I wanted to be a brickie. I did. I wanted to become a bricklayer because you got to work outdoors, you'd start early, finish at 3 pm, you could build your muscles up and I thought I'd be able to play footy, go to training and play for Canterbury-Bankstown. That's what a lot of my mates did.

However, my mother decided that was not going to be my life. I filled out a university form, because everybody in my level at school filled out a university form. I did it and didn't give it another thought. Following matriculation, I got an offer to go to university. I came home from wherever I'd been one day – probably footy training – and my mother had opened the offer letter. She said, 'We're going to enrol you.' I said, 'I don't want to go to university.' I didn't even know where the university was. I didn't know anything about universities, I had no clue what she was talking about.

Our family members were all labourers, worked in restaurants and cafés. I was going to be the first to go to university. Mum said, 'You're going to university. I'm taking you.' And so, my mother took me to the University of New South Wales in Kensington. It was like a foreign country to me. When you live in Sydney's western suburbs it's a long way to go. Back then it wasn't just geographically a long way to travel, it was a long way from what I thought I would end up doing. Mum enrolled me. First in commerce, then the commerce–law combined degree. She just said, 'This is what I think is a good thing for you.' I said, 'Okay, I'll give it a try.'

And that's how I do everything. No problem. Boxing, business, a deal with Kerry Packer, selling the business to GE, whatever. Okay. Let's do it. Let's see what happens. I'm still the same. I just take the view of,

'What's the worst thing that can happen to me?'

Mum might have pushed me to enrol in uni but what she also did was push me to rethink the box that I or others might put me in. She pushed me to think bigger and to expand my expectations. That is a big gift to give anyone. The belief that they can aim high. For me, it was time to start doing some proper thinking.

FIND YOUR POWER AND BACK YOURSELF

1. Don't let others define who you are.
2. Don't underestimate the importance of hard work.
3. Push yourself out of your comfort zone – because what's the worst that could happen?
4. Are you a cutter or a sewer? Play to your strengths.
5. Surround yourself with people who want you to succeed. It sounds simple, but if you are hanging with people who don't have your back, move on.

Building an Army

Enough looking back for a minute, we need to discuss where we're at right now. I've witnessed Australia's enormous potential being squandered as entrepreneurship is ignored, ingenuity is punished and our reputation for boxing above our weight class as a nation is torn down (and this was the case even before the pandemic too).

We've become a nation of sheep, happy to plod along in mediocrity and pray we're not devoured by a wolf.

'It's time to say, "fuck that".'

Businesses are on the brink, many already gone. Builders, real estate agents, car salespeople, hairdressers, market stall holders and the owners of restaurants, cafés, hotels, travel agents, fashion stores, clubs and pubs are all making heart-breaking decisions. If you don't know when or where the next customer dollar is coming from, or which member of staff you're going to lay off next, then the economic virus is at your door. If you've had to pull down the shutters on your business, if you've had to lay off loyal workers or if your job has vanished, then the virus has crossed your threshold. Across suburbs and regional communities, there isn't one home that hasn't been infected by this virus in Australia.

In parallel with the sufferers of the actual COVID-19 virus, the other sufferers of this pandemic are the rank and file of business – owners, workers, colleagues. They are the people who live next door, in the same apartment block or down the street. Or they are us. The grinders who have had to get smart, get crafty, get punchy, just to survive. The strivers, the improvers and the disruptors who have been getting up at 3 am to make daily, sometimes hourly, adjustments just to keep up with the new rules and restrictions.

The only way we'll beat this economic virus is if we don't pull in different directions. We don't know how we'll recover, but our best shot is to do it together.

This isn't the time for politicians to revert to partisan lines with an eye on vote-grabbing. The point-scoring has to stop. We need unity at this critical time.

Federal and state governments must work together, heading in a unified direction. No bickering, no undermining; everyone on the same page, the page that spells out our survival. We have (mostly) been unified against the health virus, now's the time for the same single-minded defiance against the economic virus.

I believe this economic virus will outlast the health virus and it will potentially destroy even more Australian livelihoods and lives. If we want – and I certainly do – that factory, that shop, that business, that job to be there next week, we need leaders to act like they mean business for our businesses. Governments have started the job, but it is just the beginning.

We need to apply the same tactics to this fatal enemy as we are applying to the health virus. It's time to find out as much about the economy as we've come to know about COVID-19. We need daily updates, a dedicated action team led by seasoned local business drivers, borders secured from foreign commercial invaders with exactly the same swiftness as we shut our entry points down at the beginning of the pandemic. We have to flatten the curve of unemployment like we flattened the curve of infection. We must look at the unemployment number every day and not let one more lost job be added to it.

Let it be our collective mantra from this day to rebuild this nation, faster than the rest of the world. Let's be the envy of all those who observe us and be an example of excellence. No one asked for this pandemic and, while the pain is inevitable, our suffering is optional.

'The system needs to change.'

I want a revolution in the way things are done. The system needs to change, or more importantly, the way people – and in particular the small business community – are represented needs to change.

I didn't get where I am by doing what everyone else does. I don't take unnecessary risks, but I do buck the system and push the parameters. You have to if you want things to change. This is a time of massive change, so I'm going to push my luck. I'm going to say what needs to be said:

'The members of the small business community
are the forgotten people of today.'

There are around 2.2 million small business owners in Australia. The number of people who have jobs in Australia is 12 million. The small business sector employs 65 per cent of those. So, you've got 2.2 million small business owners, plus 65 per cent of the 12 million (say 8 million people). Add those together and that's about 10 million. Ten million people are gainfully employed and have a purpose every single day of their life because of the small business community.

That's just over 80 per cent of the 12 million people working. That to me is why small business is the heartland of Australia.

And yet small business can never get a roll on. They can't get any momentum so that they can be heard. There's no power in *small* business. You know why? Because they call it *small* business. This suits the banks and the politicians: 'You're a *small* business owner. You've got no say.'

I want us to stop using these terms 'small' or 'medium' business. A *'crucial, vital business'* – that's what we should be calling the backbone of our economy.

You know what? Small business is the middle class of Australia – we *run the joint*. They keep everything afloat. They are the people who get up and open coffee shops at five o'clock in the morning to make the coffee. They are the ones having to change the way they operate just to survive. They're the survivors. The ones sent out to war all the time.

The people down in Canberra, they don't take a hit. Small business owners are taking the hit for them and they don't complain about it. They are not often on Twitter. They don't have time to spend bullshitting around and protesting – they're too busy. And because they're not noisy, they are too easily forgotten.

Small business, this is your call-to-arms, it's time to say: 'We want a say.'

You are the people the government should be talking to. You are the very people who need to be represented. Today.

If I ever represent anyone, it's the small business owner because that is who I feel closest to. So I'm saying, 'Let's do something about this. Let's represent you. Let's build something for you. And what about if we build something where you get a real vote?'

In the last decade or so, the finance industry has gone mental. We've had royal commissions, we've had the global financial crisis (GFC), property boom, property bust, a variety of changes in government, changes in prime minister mid-term, drought, bushfires and now the COVID-19 crisis. It's just been an incredible journey of – well, I feel as though I've been on my own personal version of *The Odyssey*. I don't know if you've read Homer's Greek epic poem, but I have. I feel that, like Odysseus, I, too, am trying to find home, the place where I want to be, and it's just one obstacle after another. From others using dodgy business practices that give us all a bad name vis-à-vis royal commissions to the screaming banshees of COVID-19. Not literally, obviously, but in a business sense it's been an incredible test for me. But I am strong and I've been around long enough to know what I have to do to get through. So I know others have been doing it really tough. The way I look at it is I'm being tested: tested to think, tested to endure, tested to not just talk about resilience but actually exercise it, tested to reinvent, tested to remain relevant, tested to – well, I guess, to overcome.

It has been a very, very gruelling but, for me, enjoyable period. I like working hard and finding solutions to problems. People always ask me, 'What are you doing it for? Why are you putting yourself through that?' Well, I'm doing it because it's in front of me. I fight for what I believe in and I fight what's in front of me. I'm not going to step around or walk away from anything just because it is difficult.

If it means I have to navigate my business through a royal commission, I will. If it means I've got to navigate myself and my business through a COVID-19 crisis, a pandemic, I will. And I enjoy it. To me that's the great thing in life.

'There's no point carrying on pretending to be some sort of warrior if you're not prepared to go to war.'

Sir Garfield Barwick – the seventh and longest serving Chief Justice of Australia – once said, 'War paint does not make the warrior.' I feel as though there are plenty of people out there today with lots of war paint on who claim to be something that they're not, but I reckon anyone who's survived in business in the last ten years – whatever the industry – really is a warrior because it's been a hard decade.

So now's the time. We need to help each other. Right now I want to build an army of business warriors from all over the country.

> 'What I'd love to be able to do is gather
> together an army of small business
> owners, small business warriors, and get
> you represented, get you heard.'

I want to get small business owners freed up and highlighted, get you some real estate. By which I mean getting you seen, getting you in everybody's perception and everybody's reality, instead of you being taken for granted. I'm not a romantic, but it's become my purpose as I get older to build this army. To share my hard-won wisdoms about business so others can benefit. Let's face it, the big players are the ones that dominate. The big players are much smaller in number, and much smaller in significance, but they get heard.

I'll give you an example. I recently listened to the prime minister talk about eight big projects that are receiving funds and being fast-tracked. These are big projects employing 46,000 people or something of that size. And I said, 'Well, that's great. But there are over two million small and medium business owners who employ eight million people, not forty-six thousand people. Eight million people who are all getting held up by some administrative bullshit.'

For example, right now, going into a café or a restaurant you have to put your phone camera on a QR code, open the QR code, open the website and register every time you go there.

The premise of these protocols is to protect everybody. And I don't want anyone getting COVID-19 so I back anything that keeps us safer, but where does it leave the small business owner? Customers go, 'Oh that's too hard.' Customers don't want to have to do that every day just to sit in a café. I don't want to do it. It's turning people off and driving people away from small business. It's red tape. There has to be a better way. While we were in lockdown, small business owners showed their innovation every day, so we need government to continue to back them and reward ingenuity. I am not seeing enough of that.

And then you hear, 'We're going to fast-track these big projects, get rid of all the red tape for these eight huge projects.' And this work is going to be done by one corporation or another, turning a small minority of people into bigger billionaires than they already are.

Small business is going to go backwards, while a very select number of big businesses are going to go forward. These administrative issues, this red tape and legislative impediments like regulated hours are going to send small businesses – and all the people in them – broke.

We need to do something. And the only way it's going to happen is if we build an army of small-to-medium size businesspeople so people will listen to them. Like Michael Jordan said, 'Talent wins games, but teamwork and intelligence win championships.'

Because, as I said before, right now small business owners are under-represented and forgotten. The hairdresser, the restaurant owner, the newsagent, the local shop keeper, the tradie, the book shop owner … you! Small business warriors out there in droves. If the government gets you onside, you'll turn the economy around in a heartbeat. The problem is you've been fed bullshit for so long and don't have anyone to believe in. There's not much, maybe a matchstick, a lit match, between small business owners feeling strong and positive and wanting to go forward, and feeling demeaned and going backwards. It would be so simple to get you really firing.

We need initiatives outside the norm. We need policy that's never been seen before. Let's focus on, for example, getting businesses cash, incentivising the private sector to employ, and bolstering consumer sentiment. They're just a few innovations, but they're never going to happen if I raise them because I don't have an army behind me.

This is where my whole recent mentor thing came from.

I have a business and a site, Mentored (mentored. com.au), devoted entirely to mentoring. Starting off, I just wanted to pay forward what I'd learned. I wanted to share some of my knowledge. But it's evolved, because small business owners are so busy and there's so much bullshit on offer. There's any one of a number of speakers you could go and listen to for $2000 or $3000. You walk out, you're all motivated and five months later you fall flat on your arse. It is not money well spent and it doesn't help anyone, except the now cashed-up speaker. I am not a fan of that.

This is not about lifestyle or personal development. This is about representation. You small business owners need to feel like you're part of something, that you count. It's being part of something, having a say, a voice, and being part of something significant in this country. A movement.

That's what I've focused my mentoring on and evolved it into.

If I can represent this army, I want to get governments to pay attention. There's no bargaining power unless we form a vocal group. Go back ten thousand years, I could have walked up to a castle and said, 'Listen, you're eating all the food that we're growing, and the crops that we're growing, and you're starving us to death,' and they'd have said, 'Well, fuck off.' But if I turn up with 17,000 men and women with swords and shields, they'll pay more fucking attention.

Nothing's changed.

That's the journey I'm on now. To get more respect and attention for small business owners. You put food on your family's table. You pay for your kids to get through school. You build jobs for others and – crucially – make communities happy.

I saw a guy the other day, a delicatessen/café owner around where I live. He was telling me how he's tired and not making that much money, and I said, 'You know what though? At the end of the day, you don't realise how important you are to the community you're in.' He owns the only coffee shop in the whole area. When you drive by you see everybody out the front, chatting. 'How are you? How are you going through all of this?' Otherwise we would never talk to each other. It's such an important community thing. That's why I'm against Uber Eats and Menulog, because they're killing all the cafés and restaurants. They're making small business owners work for them to provide product. The fact that Uber delivers to you at home stops you from going back to the place where you used to go. It kills communities. Yes, it's a great concept, and they're probably doing very well financially, but I don't like the fact that these businesses are alienating people from the community. Community is at the heart of everything. One of the things I've learned during this COVID-19 period is just how important community is. It's more important to me now than it has ever been before and I think that's everybody's attitude.

This book is about building that long overdue respect for small business and that vital representation. It's about empowering you to tell others this message. You're worried that you and your business don't have a fucking snowflake's chance in hell of surviving the next ten years. I want to make sure you do.

BE A SMALL BUSINESS WARRIOR

1. Don't avoid difficult situations – fight what you're confronted with and find a solution.

2. Learn about markets, the rules and the regulations, but don't be reined in by them if you can see better ways to work – make the system work for you.

3. Never forget how vital you are to our economy and to your local community.

4. Get ready to stand up and be heard.

5. Join up. (see p. 284)

ROUND THREE

How to Think

At one stage in my life, after learning how power works in business and in society, I thought I might end up in politics. But when I looked at that I realised that being a politician would be an ineffective and unsatisfying area to be in for someone like me, who is anti-establishment. I'm in favour of non-hypocritical authority and influence, and that's something I want to harness and work on. It seems to me politicians get caught up and compromise their beliefs to hold onto power. I'm not up for that. So I've got to do something different.

> 'I want to make change, but you
> need power to make change.'

I'm looking for a base which is powerful enough to allow me to make change for the better.

A base like my businesses, Wizard and Yellow Brick Road (YBR), to some extent has done that, which I'll come to shortly enough. Wizard was always about changing the way companies deal with people, for me it was about finding the humanity and I mean that – I was hoping that I could help people get their home, their dream. The banks weren't prepared to do it, so I did it. I'm doing it now with YBR too but in many ways we're still part of the establishment process. I mean, we're all part of the same system. You can't help people get their homes today without being part of the banking system so I'm now a part of it. We try to be nicer, kinder, more accessible. We try to be cheaper, but it's only at the margin. All of it's only at the margin, because the system won't allow anything different and I can't see my way past that system. So, for now we've worked out how to engineer ourselves into the system in such a way that we can benefit people and provide competition. When the GFC occurred people like me were told, 'You're not a bank, you haven't got a credit rating, you haven't been around one hundred years, you are not allowed back in the system like you were during the Wizard days, so you're out.'

We've spent the last ten years at YBR trying to work out how to financially engineer our way back into the

45

system without compromising our aims too much, which we've just done. It took us more than a year to complete it, we've been working on it for ten years. It's like building a rocket and flying to the moon. We are now back in the market and in the system but what's different today compared to the Wizard days is you can't do it without relying on the banking system. They let us into the system on the basis that we rely on them. You have your own product, you can make it slightly different, at the margin you can help more people at a better price, but the system still dominates the real criteria. I still love working in that space because it's a good service to the community. But now I'm also interested in doing something different and that requires radical thinking.

Convergent and divergent thinking

I want you to have the opportunity to understand a little bit about how I think, rather than what I think, because maybe it can help you to develop your own business or future.

There are essentially two ways of thinking: convergent and divergent thinking.

Convergent thinking is very mathematical because you take everything that's around you and you converge all your thoughts into one outcome. One plus one can only equal two in maths, that's the truth. Convergent thinking delivers a truth, a real truth; there's no dispute. One plus one equals two, end of story. That's why it's very mathematical. But its downside is we become compliant. We are locked into existing systems and existing ways of doing things. It is a very important aspect of business but it can exclude innovators and stymie creative thinking. Convergent thinking means tapping into the systems around us. It means thinking a certain way. A rebellion against this can see people try and question the status quo and attach a whole load of conspiracy theories to things. For example, there're a million conspiracies around COVID-19 because people seem to instinctively know that you shouldn't just think convergently but they can't quite work out what that next thinking process is.

Divergent thinking is where I give you a hundred variables and they don't equal one outcome, they equal twenty, thirty or fifty possible outcomes and finding a solution requires quite a bit of creativity. Most people don't have the right mix of convergent and divergent thinking. There seems to be either people who are artistic who just think divergently – everything they think about has got a thousand possibilities and they rarely land on anything and rarely end up doing anything. Then you've got all the people out there who just think convergently and live in a narrow world that they never move outside, and they never achieve what their underlying talents would allow them to do because they can't think divergently.

I believe to succeed you need to have a good blend of the two types of thinking. It should be taught in schools and entrenched in our kids not just to question something but to deeply consider every aspect of it so they can understand the many different aspects of a problem or issue.

It might seem a sweeping statement but from my experience, small business owners tend to think convergently because they get on the merry-go-round of the day-to-day stuff, especially regarding regulations and in particular GST, BAS and keeping the books. All of this re-orders our minds. Small business owners get up, if they have a family everyone goes off to school or childcare, they go to their shop or office or head off to a client or whatever their business is, they spend a whole day dealing with transactions or a contract or customers and focusing on whatever their business might be, they collect their money, they go and do the books and then they go to bed. The next day is the same, in some ways they are living Groundhog Day with no space for creative or divergent thinking unless they make time for that. Most people don't. And so they're just doing the same convergent thinking every day. Everything converges, everything goes into their time: breakfast time, lunchtime, transactional time, work time, partner time, kid time, sport times, exercise time, social time. That's routine and very convergent unless you also find ways to shake yourself up and give yourself space to think differently. You need time to daydream, to plan, to imagine other ways of doing things.

Now, I often talk about routine, which might sound convergent, but my routine includes time to think divergently. To me, that's my fantasy time. I'm always thinking about different ways of doing things over and above everything I do. How do I make change? What can I create? I constantly question what I am doing to see if I can do it better. I don't talk about divergent thinking very much, which is why I wanted to talk about it now, because people think I'm the person who's saying, 'Get on and do it.' People think that I'm regimented. I'm not. You can have a routine but if you let that rule everything you are going to get bogged down and lose your edge.

I want to tell you about divergent thinking because in business, your business, you need to understand it. Like everything, you need to find the time for those 'Eureka!' moments.

If you understand the idea of convergent and divergent thinking then you have the capacity to do both. But what about the person who doesn't know what they don't know? The person who only behaves with convergent thinking. How do they start thinking divergently?

You don't have to have a talent for divergent thinking, if you can understand the idea, believe in it, then you can develop a talent for divergence. It's just sitting, thinking about fanciful things. We're told to meditate and think about nothing – that's good because we are busy doing something all the time, right? Well, what about this idea:

> 'We should be told to sit down and think for half an hour about what we can do that's different.'

It doesn't matter what it is, I don't care what it is. I just want you to exercise your divergent thinking. It's really important. I do it all the time. When I was a kid I was the maddest dreamer – I don't mean in my sleep, nor dreamy in a dopey sense, 'Oh, he's such a dreamer', but I was always dreaming up ideas and just thinking about what I could do or how would I do this and how would I do that.

I loved listening to The Beatles' songs, and when I say 'listening' I don't mean I had the music on in the background. I would just lie there, close my eyes, listen to them and try to imagine what it was that they were saying and doing, or what they were thinking. We need to put this kind of thinking in the school curriculum to encourage it. We've got to develop our brains.

I love the idea of being able to help people become the best that they can be. To be the best you can be is not just about becoming the best at whatever-it-is-you-do, it's not just that. It's about you being able to think in the best way you can. This is something I'm chasing all the time. I'd like to spend the rest of my life focused on this, expressing it to other people and encouraging this to become part of us all.

Start thinking

Imagine that you walk into a small business and you can see that whoever's been running that small business has been diminished by narrow, convergent-only thinking. How can you help them turn things around?

The first thing I would do is ask a business owner this, 'Have you thought about doing it another way?' 'Have you thought about your product being delivered differently?' Or I'd give them an example of someone else who does something innovative – nothing to do with their industry – and show them how they diverged to a different approach. Maybe they sat down and they thought they were a postman but now they're working as a delivery agent for an e-commerce company and now they own the e-commerce company, or they're vertically integrating, understanding how important deliveries are relative to e-commerce.

> 'If you're thinking what business should I go into now, or if your business is tanking and you're wondering what you can do now – divergent thinking would say, "Well, what's out there?"'

What's growing? What's available? Where can I see a tide rising?

At this moment, one of the current meteoric growth areas is delivery, as a delivery agent you will be assured good business, assuming you can buy a van. You know why you can't buy a delivery van? No stock. They've all been sold. The recent pandemic's accelerated the issue but the delivery industry was growing before that.

Even so, let's run with that example. Let's say you're someone who came to me and said, 'I don't know what to do, Mark. I've always been a cook.'

And I would say, 'Okay, well can you drive a car?'

'Yeah.'

'And you've got a nice personality, a friendly personality in case someone answers the door when you do a delivery?'

'Yeah.'

'Have you got the physical ability to pack a truck or a van?'

'Yeah, I'm still young enough, I'm physical enough.' Or, 'Yeah, maybe I need to do a bit of exercise, a bit of a workout, a bit of training. Maybe work on my diet.'

'Can you follow an iPhone map? Google Maps?'

'Okay I'm pretty good at that.'

'Can you borrow some money? Have you got a bad credit history?'

'No, I don't.'

'Okay, can you borrow twenty-five thousand to buy a small van? Those Volkswagen vans, whatever they are.'

'I'm not sure.'

'Do you realise interest rates are the lowest they've been for years? Do you know who actually lends money on these things at the moment? Well, Volkswagen will lend you money to buy one of their own cars, VW Finance will, Toyota Finance.'

'No, I didn't know.'

'Okay, well have you ever thought about going to the company who's actually trying to sell you the car? They'll lend you money. Do you realise that there's a rising tide there?'

'Why is that?'

'Well, people are sitting at home, they can't make it out to the shops, they're going to buy things online. Guess what they'll be delivered in? They've got to be delivered, who's delivering this shit? It's not Australia Post. Delivery companies.'

And that way of buying won't go away. Right now the biggest issue for e-commerce is what they call fulfilment, that is getting stuff to the customer on time. There's a huge business in that.

If that were me then I would be thinking to myself, *How can I get ten vans?* Then I'm thinking, *What things would I like to get delivered?*

Right now I don't like going to the supermarket. And I don't want to go to the fruit and veg shop at the moment. I have to buy online because I no longer want to go to the shops. So, wouldn't it be good as a delivery person if I bought a refrigerated van and I started delivering parcels. Maybe I could pack it up with fruit and then I could become a franchisee of the fruit and veg people in my local area.

I've thought about this and if I could get five people to do it, over time everyone would know about us. Then we could park the van in the street like the old Mr Whippy truck used to do, maybe have some music, and open up the van. The fruit and veg would all be laid out, everybody would walk up there after four or five o'clock because everyone's working from home now and they'd come and select their fruit. They wouldn't have to go to the fruit store, they'd come out, just the local neighbourhood, and buy the fruit and veg. You could do it with fish, you could do it with meat. Right now you are forced to go to people's shops online but I think that the vendor should take it offline and come to you in your street. Then you can just walk up. If I were the vendor I would go from street to street so there's a schedule. At 4 pm I'll be in this street, 6 pm in that street, 7 pm in the next street and 8 pm in that street, 6 am tomorrow morning in this street. I can do five streets a day, seven days a week, that's thirty-five streets. There's my franchise.

This is kind of what it used to be like back in the sixties when I was growing up. We're going back to the bread, milk and the drink van. The drink van. That's the ultimate customer service. Customers want ultimate customer service. I'm a customer, I want service.

'Everyone's forcing us to buy the way that they want us to buy. They think we've got nowhere else to go.'

But someone can just take it offline and away from the shop and take it right to your street. And what if I do this and I use data and artificial intelligence to work out which streets I need to be at, at what time? Over time, over three months, I will know where I make the best sales, what I sell there, and what I need to put in my van. I can just buy some software off the shelf and it will tell me my best streets, what I sell most of, my most expensive items, at what times and which streets in these franchises. That's divergent thinking.

> 'I don't believe people know how to think properly. I don't believe people think about pushing their thoughts into reality.'

There's no thought process going into how we think. We know how to do yoga and we know how to do Pilates and aerobics. I know how to lift a weight. I know all the physical things. I know to take vitamin B complex and vitamin C, but we don't know how to think for ourselves.

It seems schools and universities today teach people what to think. Not how to think. What to think is different to how to think. When I first went to university, especially the University of New South Wales, it was based on the Socratic method of teaching. It's not anymore. The University of New South Wales was ahead of the rest in terms of how they taught students to think. They didn't have lectures. Whereas at the University of Sydney, you'd turn up to university, sit in a lecture theatre and the lecture was delivered to you. You wrote notes. You were being told what to think, what your content needed to be.

The University of New South Wales had tutorials instead of lectures. In a tutorial they never told you anything, they asked you questions and you had to answer. That's the Socratic method. They don't do it anymore but they did it initially. It was a big thing – a Harvard-style university. It's telling you what to think but it's also telling you how to think. There's not enough how to think today. Right now we are getting told what to think; our mobile phones do it to us, because they're all content. It's everybody else's process and we are becoming extremely convergent.

This isn't hard stuff. It's easy to think. To learn how to think. That's why people look to me on Mentored, my mentor project. It's not about telling people what to do, it's about asking questions and having people work out for themselves what to do. I am against spoon-feeding people. We are spoon-fed all day, all night about everything. All our leaders are spoon-feeding us every minute of the day. Premiers, prime ministers, presidents – they're all doing it. And most of it's bullshit but we're not questioning it. They can get away with spin and hypocrisy because too many of us are not thinking about what we are being told. I'm not talking about becoming a conspiracy theorist. I am talking about using your mind to question and analyse facts and science and figures and then having the thought processes that enable you to push back.

> 'We are being spoon-fed, we're all gulping it down. No one's saying, "Wait a minute."'

The only people who are not being spoon-fed at the moment are radicals, the splinter groups, but they're anti-whatever-everybody-else-says. They're not necessarily divergent thinkers, they're just against everything. That's no good either. They're against the mainstream. But the problem is that we, the mainstream, are letting this happen to us because we don't know how to think. It's a big deal for me. It's a really big deal.

It's not only about needing to think, you must go back to how to think. We all need to take a break and start thinking – about anything and everything. I don't give a fuck what you think about; whether it's your industry or any other industry.

> 'Just think on this one question: Where's the rising tide in commerce today? What am I experiencing, what am I seeing?'

You don't have to have read a hundred books, you don't have to have read *The Economist* or the *Financial Times*. You don't have to have read any of that stuff, although the more you read, the more ideas and the more exposure to ideas you get. But for now, just have a look around you, close your eyes and think, *Where's the tide rising?*

As I said, there's an easy answer to this question right now. Delivery, couriers. It's a really simple answer. E-commerce requires a fulfilment of e-commerce. There're places you can go beyond that, you can say, 'Well, maybe there's a box that I could invent that could go in the front of people's houses. It's an electronic box and allows the courier to put the delivery in there, safe and secure, and the box then sends a message to the e-merchant and another message to the customer to tell them that something's just been delivered.' There's a million variations on this. My wish is that people will start thinking. And I want to help them do it. It is not about mindfulness or visualisation. It is more abstract and free flowing. It is about exploration.

It's not about creativity as the end result, I don't want anyone to go down that rabbit hole because there's a whole lot of other stuff down there. It's not creating something, it's just about thinking about the possibilities.

Generally speaking, people only start thinking like this when they're in the shit. Usually that's too late. I want people to think about what the possibilities are, in anything. At any time. I want those neurological connections to get developed. There's a book called *Neurocomic*, written by neuroscientists Dr Matteo Farinella and Dr Hana Roš in collaboration with a comic illustrator. The book illustrates a neuroscientist's view of how the brain develops and how the neurological connections we all have build up a story about who we are. We develop a story. We start to live like that and it reinforces this story in our own brain and that's who we become, that person. Forever. Go read it!

'You can change that. You can make a decision. I'm not going to be that person and I'm going to be someone else.'

You can make a conscious decision and you can start developing neurologically differently to become that other person, that other being. You can change. My experience, however, is that people only do this under extreme pressure, when there's no other choice.

'Be the person who can get ahead of that before the bad stuff happens.'

60

Based on the plasticity of your brain, if you want to make a change – not because you have to make a change – or you want to make a slight detour into another path, if you're aware of this, *Neurocomic* is a great book, very easy to read. If you read it you'll understand. You'll think, *Oh, shit hang on, I can become something else if I want to.* That's an example of divergent thinking. It's about possibilities. But to do that you need to understand a little bit more about the thinking process.

In terms of who I am and what I want to do in the last stanza of my life – I want to share this thinking but I also want to make sure that I think this way more and more myself. I'm hoping that by developing this thinking I can create something that can make a difference to the world, even if it is just in the way that people think. I want to leave something behind that's permanent. I don't yet know exactly how that's going to look, or what it is – I'm still working on it. And even if I don't manage to deliver, I want to keep thinking this way until the day I die.

A good example of what I'm talking about is the life lived by the brilliant Stephen Hawking. His brain just sat there thinking about this shit all day long, every day and all night, even as disease took hold and his body atrophied. Every day he was free of his body because his mind processed endless possibilities. Challenging Einstein. The theory of relativity versus quantum mechanics. The Big Bang Theory, everything. He just thought, thought, thought and looked at all the possibilities. It's a huge privilege to be able to think about what the options in life are. It's quite rewarding to sit down and think about opportunities and alternative outcomes.

It's just an exercise. To me it's an unemotional exercise. I invite you to make this kind of divergent thinking a part of your day or part of your week. Allocate some time to it. The first thing you should do in the morning is get up, have your coffee, plan your day and read something new, something that's got nothing to do with what you ordinarily would read. It could be anything. If you're not in economics you might want to think about reading about the economy. I don't mean read the newspaper, read some magazine or text, just get your brain stimulated.

You've also got to work on the physical side of things too. If you currently don't do anything for your body, then start doing something today.

I often talk about physical routines but what I haven't talked about until now is that I also set aside some time to dream. I do it a lot. I wander round. I'm allowing myself to think about other stuff, *Maybe I might try that out?* I'm always looking around, thinking about opportunities.

> 'Try and trick your mind to travel a path that
> you wouldn't normally think of going down.'

It's become a habit for me now. It doesn't send me crazy, going down into a weird rabbit hole, chasing shit. To me it is part of the structure of my day. Even though my mind is wandering, it's also constrained. In other words, it doesn't go too far, it just happens during that allocated time.

> 'If we always do what we've always done, or if
> we always think what we've always thought,
> we'll always get what we've always got.'

It's a really weird question to ask yourself: 'How can someone think when they haven't been thinking about thinking?' Mentoring is a little bit that way too. What I'm trying to do with my mentor business is to actually put ideas in people's heads. I'm not trying to tell you what to think, I'm trying to tell you *how* to think. In actual fact, I'm telling you to just think. It's hard to say it, but by reading this book I'm sure that you'll get it.

Learn how to think

We talk about mindfulness but what about a consciousness about how we think? Being clear on what we're thinking, convergently and divergently.

I don't like that left brain, right brain definition, it doesn't make sense to me. It's become a slick sound bite. Left brain, right brain. I'd rather people move beyond that and ask, 'How can my brain work to give me a good way of thinking?' I mean the left and the right work together and there needs to be balance. Everyone's got a different balance. Just like we've all got different centres of gravity based on our height, our weight and our build. We've all got a different balance in our mind.

I'm constantly thinking and exercising my own mind, trying to build the right balance between the two styles of thinking. The balance will change and evolve, but I hope to work out a brand-new way of talking about it, a permanent change to the way we do things. Even if I can just get people to recognise that their day needs to have some fantasy in it, some divergent thinking.

Sticking to convergent thinking is a way of controlling you. What influencers really do, like many of our leaders today, they're getting you to think on one outcome.

There are people who will get us to think the way they want us to think and what you need to do is think about the outcome you want to achieve. You may want to keep doing exactly the same thing and that's fine if it makes you happy. But I just want everyone to register the fact that there may be another way of doing things, of working, of living, there may be ten other ways. Ten other possibilities. I want people to think about that and apply it to how they live their lives and how they run a business. Don't be a sheep and do the same thing because you think you should or someone tells you that you should. If you look at that in relation to how we do business then people ask, 'Well, what's going to happen with the markets?' I don't know, but think about all the possibilities. Just think about them.

Some of the big e-commerce businesses had to think that way.

I did that with my business, found other possibilities. I've got a business now called Mentor Media, which is a production business. We produce podcasts. Podcasts have been around for about ten years and have become more prevalent in the last three years. Another new rising tide. All of a sudden the number of people who want to do a podcast has increased enormously.

If you sit back and think about it, there are so many podcasts out there. How do you go about creating a podcast? Well, people try it themselves and find that the big thing about podcasts is in the editing – it's hard to do and takes expertise. People struggle to edit their own podcasts, they spend days trying to do it, it's a difficult thing. The people who are actually doing the podcast – the talent – they don't have the objectivity to look at their own stuff and be able to edit it. 'How did that sound?' 'Did I really say that?' 'Do I actually sound like that?' You need a third party to edit your work and most times they can do it much more efficiently.

It's important that you don't ever put yourself into a box that you never step out of. Say you trained as a graphic designer, but then there're not many jobs. The marketplace for the traditional graphic designer job is shrinking. But if you know how to use a camera, you can turn your talent for graphics to your advantage. You can produce things with your visual vocabulary. You know how to use a camera and you can learn how to edit images and you could start building your own visual media business and enhance content to go alongside podcasts.

I came up with the idea of doing a podcast for myself, which I now do weekly, but I knew jack shit about producing the show. I had no idea and yet I've taken my business into podcast production. I've learned. We're now inundated by requests to help others do the same. We're building a podcast studio for dedicated people wanting to do their own. It's called the Podcast Collective, so people can go in there and just focus on getting their podcast right.

Who would have thought podcasting would become a business arm of mine? At Mentor Media we've gone from zero to producing nine, ten podcasts a month, the beginning of an upward curve. We make good money, it's an extra stream of income. So that's an example of divergent thinking delivering a new business. It's a side hustle that came from divergent thinking but not at the expense of my core businesses.

•

With divergent thinking in business, you have to be able to divorce yourself from things you like, or that mean something to you, when you're grazing for opportunity.

'Consider all the possibilities and then determine which ones are doable based on your own resources and skills.'

Do your hustle on the side

If you're not desperate and you're making money out of what you currently do, don't sit around pondering all the possibilities and butchering what you're currently doing, which is making you money. But at five o'clock you should say, 'I'm going to stop that business, my normal business, and I'll do my pondering. And after that I'll do my planning and my thinking and my researching.' Because once you consider the possibilities, then you need to go and do some hard research to put something solid behind your ideas.

This is what people typically call the side hustle. People who do side hustles are people who are good at divergent thinking.

A side hustle is exactly as it sounds, something you do on the side. But for me, you only ever do it after-hours. You never murder the thing that's paying you a living. Never. Do your hustle on the side.

And those opportunities will only come about after you have thought about the possibilities and found a rising tide.

•

The thing to remember is that change is the only constant and you have to be ready to act and think of possibilities and opportunities so when the moment is right you are ready. But sometimes all the divergent thinking and all the hard graft might not bring the results you want.

People come to me for solutions all the time: 'Mark, what's the solution to [whatever their problem is]?' I don't know what the solution is for most people but I might be able to think about the possibilities, because I employ this discipline of how to think. I've used this discipline with all of my businesses and I am the first to admit not everything has been a success. Sometimes I've had to say, 'Fuck, I can't really think of any solution. I'm out.' But I have always made sure I looked at all the angles first.

I was involved in a business some years ago, a property development business where we acquired a whole lot of hotels, like the Sheraton Hotel in Noosa and the InterContinental in Double Bay, Sydney. Then the GFC hit and, no matter what we tried to do, we couldn't get around the fact that we needed to borrow money. But, because of the GFC, no one was going to give us any money. I left the company because I couldn't see how I could change things. I said to everyone, 'I'm out because I know I can't make any difference here.' My partners weren't ready to give up. They persevered with new partners and stayed on for a couple of years but in the end they had to put the business into administration and someone else came and took it over. They ran out of time.

But I just knew – the GFC was here, I knew what the banks were going to say, they were not going to lend us the money to fund the construction of these buildings and, no matter what I tried to imagine or dream, there was just no way out. The business needed liquidity and the GFC meant global liquidity was non-existent. I did all I could to think of ways around the problem but I couldn't see any solution. So, that's when you have to be smart and find yourself another possibility. And I did just that. I launched Yellow Brick Road, which I will talk more about later in this book. But the lessons I learned about divergent thinking helped me deal with setbacks and find new business opportunities. All because when I was a kid, I didn't lock myself into convergent thinking and I gave myself time to dream.

GET YOUR THINKING RIGHT

1. Routine isn't bad, unless it makes you rigid and unable to give yourself time to think expansively. You need time to daydream, think freely and let your mind run.

2. Mix up what you read, watch and listen to. Listen to podcasts about history or business or watch documentaries that will exercise your brain.

3. Exercise your body, too. When I hit the gym or the boxing ring, I am not only focusing on the physical benefits, I am also unlocking my mind from the mundane everyday and in doing that I can find divergent thinking time.

4. To make change happen, look at side hustles and explore possibilities before you make any extreme decisions about a new business.

5. Pay attention. Focus on what is happening in your community and in the world and let your thoughts take you places and test out theories. Be brave and bold and don't let others limit your daydreaming.

ROUND FOUR

Taking Them On

It wasn't a conscious thought of mine to go to university, but my mum pushed me in that direction and my attitude in those days wasn't to buck what was expected of me. I enrolled and took it from there.

At that time, I was used to a lot of structure in my life. I used to go to school very early because anyone who did higher levels at school had to do extra classes at 7 am. The way I lived was very structured and I liked that. I also played footy and had training at certain times. I was this young bloke and there was a time and a place to do everything. Suddenly, when I went to uni, my time was my own. I wasn't used to that.

I was travelling from Punchbowl to Kensington every day. Time on public transport might have given me the space for divergent thinking but I wasn't focused on that then. I wanted to get places quickly, so I went and bought a car, it cost me 200 bucks. I bought it from a wrecking yard. It was an old Holden HD and on one side there was a panel missing – the whole panel over the wheel – I put nothing in its place for a long time. But that car was mine and it got me where I needed to be.

My parents made me work every summer holidays. I had to work in the factory my dad worked in, and I had to give 30 per cent of everything I earned to my mum. She would spend that money on an item for the house, like a sideboard or something, so I could see where my money went. Thirty per cent out of my hard-earned wage and I happily gave it to her.

The other 70 per cent was mine. It wasn't much money, because I was labouring as either a process worker or factory worker and the pay wasn't big. I also worked with my dad, cleaning offices. My dad had a cleaning job two nights a week on top of his daytime job. I started helping him clean from about the age of twelve. We were emptying ashtrays and garbage tins, vacuum-cleaning the floor, scrubbing the toilets and stuff like that. I would get five bucks for that.

Even with my car, travelling across Sydney to uni every day became a bit too hard, so I ended up moving closer to the university. We had a six-month semester in those days, with two semesters a year, and you could either turn up to the tutorials or not, it was up to you. I was doing subjects that I hadn't done at school. I hadn't done economics or anything like that but part of the commerce degree I was doing was economics commerce. I didn't know about commerce. I had no idea what they were talking about in tutorials. No idea what I was doing. Business law subjects were also totally foreign to me, so I didn't turn up to tutorials because there was no compulsion to do it.

This was the first point in my life where doing something was optional. I was used to a tight framework, where I knew there would be some consequences if I didn't turn up for things. It suited me. The idea of freedom was a new concept to me.

Not many of my friends from school went to university. They went off and did other things. There were some kids from my school who went to the same university, but they weren't from my group of friends. So I didn't have any friends once I got to uni. They were mostly kids from the eastern suburbs. I wasn't hanging out with the rugby league guys, because I couldn't get to training, and so I had no rugby league friends either.

I found it difficult to make new friends. It looked like everybody else was always in groups. They used to go to coffee shops and I had never drunk coffee in my life, even though I'd come from a Greek home. Mum and Dad drank tea. Going to coffee shops wasn't my thing. I didn't think I could go up and start talking to these guys and get friendly. I didn't know how to get friendly. I had a couple of guys and girls who I knew to say hello to, but that was it.

I was doing four subjects in that first semester and I failed two of them. I'd never failed in anything – at school or in my life.

The reason I failed was because I thought I could study just before the exams and not go to the tutorials. This is what I had always done at school, but this time it didn't work. I was meant to hand things in, I was meant to go to tutorials – and I didn't do any of that. I didn't have a system. I didn't have a clue about university life.

Eventually I got a letter from the university, which read, 'Not only do you have to do the four subjects you have to do in the second semester, which is mandatory, but you have to repeat two subjects. You have to do six subjects in the second semester. If you fail one of those two subjects that you've already failed, you're out. You're finished.'

I'd won a scholarship and a bursary, so they were paying me money to go to university, and suddenly I'm holding this letter in my hands!

I shat myself, I thought, *This is a big deal.*

That letter jerked me awake pretty quick. Like, *Oh fuck, I'm going to have a real problem here. I'm going to get kicked out of university.* There were going to be consequences.

University had been a big life change. Everything was different and it was all up to me what I did or didn't do. And it threw me. I didn't realise the toll it was taking on me.

I didn't know what to do but I knew I had to do something. I didn't have support from my mum and dad – not to blame them, I just didn't talk to them about it. It wasn't a conversation I knew how to have with them.

I went to a doctor and talked through how I was feeling. He put me on an antidepressant. I was depressed but I hadn't been able to name it up until that point. I'd never been depressed in my life. Now I understood and it was a relief. I started to get my head right again. I'd been so disorientated. I was only seventeen when I went to university. Most kids turn eighteen in Year 12 but I had only turned seventeen in my last school year, so I was really young. I look back and I realise how immature I was.

I wasn't a social person. I never have been. My mates would ring me and say, 'Let's go out, we're going to walk around the area, or catch a bus somewhere.' I would just stay home. I'd play footy with them but I didn't really hang out with them.

My interest was in competitive activities. The only thing that motivated me to do well at school was because I wanted to compete. I wanted to be smarter than everyone else. I wanted to be in the top four, top five in the class. I wasn't studious, I just wanted to beat people. Same with footy. I would try and do everything, go for the extra training runs, because I wanted to be the best in the team. I wanted to be better than everyone else.

But because I didn't really know the other kids at uni that competitiveness didn't motivate me in the same way. The depression also took the edge off and I didn't care as much about anything.

I failed one of my exams because I was a half-hour late after my car broke down. I ran out of petrol. I'll be honest, I was a little bit absent-minded that first semester, thrown because I no longer had structure in my life. I didn't plan anything. Rather than say, 'Right, I've got to plan my day, I've got an exam tomorrow, I'd better fill my car with petrol,' I did nothing.

It was a pivotal moment for me. I still remember the spot where the car stopped. I had to walk to a service station, buy a jerry can, fill it up with petrol, take it back to the car, put it in my car, and it was just enough petrol to get me to the university. By the time I got there, the exam had already begun. I didn't have enough time to finish the exam but I was reliant on scholarship money so I had to pass. It was so stressful and I thought, *This is not going to happen again.* So, I changed things. I moved to the eastern suburbs to be closer to university and I started making an effort to plan ahead and organise myself better.

Even today I am not great at the mundane details. I leave my car running sometimes. I don't mean to, I get out of the car thinking about something I've got to do upstairs and I forget to turn the car off. I have moved off in my head before I have finished with the day-to-day details. So now I appoint people to do the planning for me. I've worked out that I'm no good at it. I don't look at my own diary, I have someone do it for me. That's a luxury I have worked hard for, but it is also about knowing what your strengths and weaknesses are, and offsetting the weaknesses when you can.

I employ another strategy to compensate for this, too. I wear the same thing every day, eat the same breakfast every morning so that I don't have to think about those things, the choices are already made, I don't have to think about the small things, which frees my mind to think bigger.

'Have a daily regime, because if you don't
do that, you'll forget something.'

I've often gone to the shops and left my car in the drive in the car park, with the engine running and all the doors open. Then I forget where I've parked my car because I wasn't thinking about what I was doing at that moment. I've got about 500 tabs open in my head at any given point. It is the complete opposite of mindfulness, but that's me.

But back to those uni days. I had a girlfriend at that stage who had been a year below me at school. We moved into a one-bedroom apartment in Bondi Road, above a famous gym called Paul Graham's Gym, across the road from the Royal Hotel. Bondi was a shithole in those days. We lived in this tiny apartment and it was twenty-nine dollars a week.

How did I feel, with all of this change taking place? Once I dealt with the depression and started to take charge of myself a bit more I came to realise I'm not a very emotional person. I experience emotions of course, but I'm not somebody who readily shares my feelings or reveals what I'm thinking. It's just the way I am.

So, at that point in my life, moving away from the western suburbs, from home, from everything I'd ever known, I didn't feel like, *Oh, wow, I'm independent.* I didn't think any of that. It was just another thing that was happening. It was just me rolling with the way life was panning out once again. But something had to give.

The dog in the night lesson

One night recently, I was at my friend's place. They have a dog, a little pup, and it wouldn't go to sleep. It was upset for some reason. At about 12.30 am, the dog started making too much noise. My friend lives in an apartment so people might have been concerned and irate about the noise. I said, 'Look, I'll take the dog back to my house.'

I was driving the dog home at 12.30 am and I was thinking about all the things I had to do and all the meetings I had lined up. A thought went through my mind, *Oh fuck, I'm going to be tired because of this incident with the dog in the night.* He might not sleep at my place either. But the thought that followed was:

'This is what I'm doing right now and I'll think about that other shit tomorrow.'

I went home. The dog must've eaten something during the day because it had bad stomach pains. It did a big crap and then had diarrhoea. It woke up every hour and I had to go and let it out. Six times I let it out.

Every time I got back to bed, I'd just be trying to get back to sleep and the dog would wake up again. And I'd think, *It doesn't really matter. I'm doing this now. I'll worry about that other stuff later.* So, I don't get stressed out by stuff like that. There's no point in worrying about what hasn't happened.

•

Don't complain

Situations like mine with the dog and the letter I received early on at university remind me of a favourite quote and philosophy from the American poet and civil rights activist, Maya Angelou: 'If you don't like something, change it. If you can't change it, change your attitude.' This message rings true in so many aspects of my life. If you're willing to complain about something, then you must be willing to take action. Otherwise, quit your whining.

Complaining is simply the product of someone who doesn't want to take responsibility, who is procrastinating or is afraid to take action. It deserves to be called out.

If you find yourself in a situation that you don't like and you feel as though you can't change that situation, try focusing your energy on whatever positives you can find. Focusing on the negatives will only tax you of your energy and that is what we must all strive to avoid. Your energy is so important and, God knows, it can be spent on more important things than complaining.

•

When I moved out of home from Punchbowl, my thinking was, *This is what I'm doing now.* All right, I won't see Mum, I won't see Dad because they're a long way away. But I'm with my girlfriend, I'm living in Bondi. I'm going to uni, that's what I'm doing now. That's how I operate.

I studied. I turned up to all the tutorials, I handed everything in I needed to hand in. I did the reading, I did what I had to do and at the end of the next semester, not only did I pass all the subjects, I got some high distinctions and a distinction average. I got another letter from university, this time saying, 'We want you to enrol in the honours degree.'

Between that first letter and the second, I worked hard and changed my attitude. It was all it took.

•

Then I started to get competitive at university and I started doing very well. I wanted to win, I wanted to get the highest mark in the subject.

I never thought about careers though. Never. All the big firms were coming out to the university and offering people jobs. I didn't even know how to apply. You had to go to these events – Deloittes would be there and Price Waterhouse. I didn't have a clue about them. I was just doing my thing, just going to university, studying.

When I was twenty, I was one of the youngest people ever to graduate from the University of New South Wales in a commerce degree. With merit as well.

My girlfriend and I had decided to get married. Why? I can't tell you. I never thought it through. I didn't even discuss it with my mum and dad. I just said, 'Mum and everyone, hello, I'm going to get married.' And they never said yes or no. They said, 'Oh, okay. Do whatever you think.'

I was the first of all my friends from school to get married. My girlfriend and I married young, only to divorce about four years later. She worked at a beauty salon when we got married. I thought I'd better get a job too. I started doing my law degree part-time at night, and I applied for a full-time job at an accounting firm. I had no idea of the difference between public accountants, chartered accountants, CPAs – I didn't have a clue. It was the first interview I'd ever been to and I didn't even wear a suit to it because I didn't own one. Nonetheless, I got the job. They told me that when I turned up for work, I'd need to wear a suit.

I'd never worn a suit in my life, apart from when I had to partner my cousins at the Greek Young Matrons' Ball. I did a few of those because I was the older cousin so I had to take my younger female cousins to the ball. We had to learn Greek dancing and present ourselves to the archbishop at the old Wentworth Hotel in Sydney. But I never actually owned a suit, we used to hire one. My mum and dad couldn't tell me anything about what kind of suit I should wear to work, all I knew was I thought I'd better go buy one.

I went to a place called Pineapple Joe. It was in the Queen Victoria building before it became the QVB, as it is now – back then it was just a row of shops. I had no idea you could buy a suit off the rack, I thought you got someone to make you one. I picked the fabric. It was light green. Light green! Not olive green, but a light, juicy-looking green. And I got the suit maker to make me a brown shirt as well, and I got a tie. I can't remember what tie I had, but I also had some brown shoes and brown socks.

I'd turn up to work in this green suit. I'll never forget it. I thought it looked pretty good. I didn't think you needed more than one suit. I had a couple of brown shirts and I'd be rushing around getting them all washed. I did all the washing myself and then on the weekend I'd take the suit to the one-hour dry-cleaning place and then put it back on the next week. I wore this green suit for months. Who knows what everyone was thinking about me? I had no clue. But I had a job and a suit.

One day, my boss told me to go into town to the Land Titles Office to get a document stamped and, as I was walking through Hyde Park, a bird shat on my shoulder. Now there was a big greasy bird shit on my green suit. I thought, *Fuck, what am I going to do here?* It was a massive stain. I took it to the dry-cleaner and they said they couldn't fix it. I went back to work. They said, 'Look, why don't you buy yourself a blue suit, a navy blue suit. We've all got navy blue suits. Go get one.' They said, 'Get two.'

I went and bought those navy blue suits. I still had the brown shoes, but it didn't matter, because now I had two navy blue suits and I was one of them. I was in my early twenties then. Twenty years later, when I was forty, I was awarded Best Dressed Man in Australia by *MODE* and *Vogue*. I wonder what they would have made of my green suit.

'I only learned how to dress by watching other
people and seeing how it was all done.'

•

I wasn't ambitious when I worked at that accounting firm. I worked hard, did a good job, but I felt like I could earn more money. One of the partners of the firm had what I thought was a really cool Fiat. I'd never seen a Fiat in my life. Everyone I knew had a Holden or Ford Falcons. I started to realise that there were people out there who had different lives, maybe better lives; better things. And the way they got them was because they were earning good money. Well, it seemed to be good money relative to what I was earning. I realised that maybe I should be trying to earn more money. I started looking in the papers and I saw a job advertised at an accounting firm in the city.

I didn't realise there were all these rankings in accounting. You've got junior fucking blah, blah, blah, partner, manager, supervisor, partner of business. Anyway, the ad was for a manager and I thought, *I can do that, that must be me.* I'd only been working for a year. I don't know why I thought it was my job, but anyway, I applied for it, wrote a letter, sent it off to the partner of the firm. The guy interviewed me. He said, 'You're not a manager, you don't have the qualifications.' Then he said, 'But, look, I've got another job for you. There's work at the firm down the road here.' Although I was naive in some areas, I certainly didn't lack in ambition. Three years later, I took over that firm.

But first, I took the junior job. My new accounting firm had a connection with a big law firm for whom we did a lot of really intricate banking, planning and structuring work. We had big business clients, particularly mining companies. I always become a student of whatever I'm doing at the time, it's my way. My area was mining and mining tax in particular. The mining tax was very complex, relatively speaking in those days anyway. There were special rules that applied to mining companies because they were trying to incentivise mining companies to do what they were doing. Not many people understood it, not many people were interested in it to be honest with you. It was a bit weird to most people, but I thought it was interesting and I became an expert in it. No one knew I was an expert other than me.

I'd never been overseas before, but when I was in my early twenties and had been working at the accounting firm for maybe a year, maybe two, I was offered the opportunity to go to Singapore to a conference. I stayed at the Shangri-La Hotel. The Shangri-La Hotel back then, this was forty years ago, it was the number one hotel in the world. I'd never in my wildest dreams ever seen anything like it.

I went to the conference and one of the topics that I went to listen to was a session on mining. I didn't know that this one conference presentation was about to alter my life. But I was ready for it.

Preparation is everything

There was a very famous accounting and law firm in those days called Greenwood Challoner. The senior tax partner of that firm was doing the conference presentation with a colleague. It lasted forty-five minutes. At the end of it, they asked, 'Are there are any questions?' And because I'd made myself an expert in this specific field, I knew the material backwards.

I could tell you every section and every subsection of the Tax Act at the time. I knew every word. I knew what went before the word, what went after the word, and the conjugation of the sentence and how the construction had been interpreted by the cases. I knew everything about it.

I used to inhale this stuff. I would sit down and read these sections one hundred and fifty times just to work out what they were trying to say. And then I'd go back to Hansard and I'd see what the draftperson's intention was and see the difference between the intention and the construction. Why I did this I've got no idea, I just did it. Even thinking about it now, I don't even know why I did it. I wasn't trying to do or prove anything. I just did it. I was interested, I guess.

And on this day, at this session of the conference, that zeal of mine paid off.

I put my hand up, I had a question. I began, 'When you were talking about section 124, large A, large H, subsection one, you said, blah, blah, blah, blah, blah.' I said this to the senior partner and he said, 'That's right,' to which I said, 'I don't agree with you.'

I was twenty-three, he would have been closer to forty-three and the number one guy in Australia in this specific field. He replied, 'What do you mean you don't agree with that?' I said, 'Well, based on this case and this particular judge in the judgement, I think that's how it would be interpreted today.' He didn't have an answer for that. He said, 'That's a good point, why don't you talk to me about it after the conference?'

What I didn't realise at the time was I had trapped him and he didn't want to be embarrassed, not in that very public situation. Either that or he didn't have an answer.

After the conference finished, that man found me. He asked me what my name was, where I was from and what I was doing. I told him. And he said, 'When you get back to Sydney, I want you to come and see me. I want to offer you a job.'

I went and saw him when I got back and he did offer me a job but I decided to stay where I was because I didn't want to join a big firm. Greenwood Challoner had heaps of partners and were a massive firm across the country and that's just not my thing.

•

I realised immediately that I knew something about this area that others didn't know, and I got a little bit ahead of myself. I was very fortunate that the law firm, Symonds and Baffsky, that my accounting firm worked with were a very famous law firm in Australia and they were acting for somebody in a test case, which became a famous tax case.

The case was called Westraders' case and it was before Sir Garfield Barwick, Chief Justice of the High Court. Symonds and Baffsky were representing the Westraders case. The QC was a guy called Russell Bainton, a very famous QC in taxation at the time.

How to stage a coup (and why I wish I hadn't)

The law firm got me to do a lot of research for them at the accounting firm I was at. I didn't realise it at the time, but I was good at research because I'd read everything over and over and over and over again, and I would deconstruct it, deconstruct it, and then reconstruct it. They got me to do a lot of research. This was in my third year of being in the job. When the judgement was being handed down in Canberra at the High Court for the Westraders case, I got invited to fly down in a Lear jet. I was twenty-three years of age and I was to be there when the judgement was being handed down along with the senior counsel, the QC, plus the senior partner from our accounting firm.

At that stage I was just a young bloke in the firm, and I was getting to meet all these incredibly senior people. We won the case and I was part of it, and all of a sudden, these people at the law firm started to say, 'Leave the accounting firm and come work for us.' I decided, no, I was going to stay where I was. Then the accounting firm offered me a junior partnership.

I took the junior partnership and after six months I said to the other junior partners, 'You know what? I'm actually smarter than all the senior partners.' This is where I got ahead of myself. I felt like I was smarter because I knew more about the legislation. I knew I was getting asked to go to things when the senior partners weren't. I knew that my work was billing more than they were billing. So I got all the young partners who had been appointed around the same time as me together and I held a meeting in the Grotta Capri restaurant.

'*Timeo Danaos et dona ferentes.*'

Virgil wrote that in the *Aeneid* over 2000 years ago. He was talking about the Trojan Horse. The Latin phrase translates into 'Beware of Greeks bearing gifts'.

Grotta Capri was a Greek restaurant in Kensington and I hired a room at the back. The guy who had first given me a run at this firm as an employee when I didn't qualify for the manager job had left the firm, but I rang him and asked him to come along too. He was much older than me. I sat down with him and all these junior partners and said, 'You know what? We're getting ripped off by these senior partners. We're doing all the fucking work.'

Now this is typical of how accounting firms and law firms work today, and it's always been the case. You get the young people, you bring them in and they work their arses off. They do it for fifteen years, and eventually they become the senior partners and then they bring in young men and women who work their arses off and so the cycle is repeated. That's the business model.

But I didn't like this business model and I thought, *Fuck that.*

So I said, 'What we're going to do is we're going to take over the firm.' I was about twenty-five by this time.

The others were older than me. They looked at me and said, 'You fucking weirdo.'

I said, 'We're going to do it,' and they said, 'How?'

'We're just going to take over,' I said.

'Well, we can't buy the firm, we haven't got any money.'

'You don't need to buy it,' I said. 'The clients make the choice where they go and we're the ones who talk to the clients, not the senior partners. They spend all their time working on some computer program.'

Computer programs were in their infancy then. The senior partners were working on this thing for a client called Prime Computing, who had a computer program they were building.

I said, 'We're out there working with the clients, we're earning all the money. They take the lion's share of the money and we only get a small percentage of the dough. We might as well have it all for ourselves and they can fuck off.'

The others asked, 'Well, how are you going to do it?'

'I'll tell you what I'm going to do. We're going to hold a cocktail party. I'm going to send a letter out to all our clients, and we'll hold the cocktail party at the Wentworth. The senior partners won't even know about it.' In those days there were no emails, no mobile phones. 'We're going to tell all our clients that we're now the firm owners, and we're going to change the name to Bouris, Dowd and Vince.' The guy who employed me originally was Paul Dowd and Geoff Vince was another young partner.

They said, 'You're fucking mad.'

'Okay, well, I'm going to get the client list. Get all the phone numbers and type a letter, and I'm going to send it to every client, inviting them to the cocktail party. We're going to announce it.'

The cocktail party was on the following Friday night and all the clients turned up. 'What's going on?' they asked.

'We've taken over the firm.'

People were saying, 'Well, congratulations. Well done, so young.'

I changed the locks on the office doors. Changed the signage. Monday morning, the senior partners turned up and couldn't get in. They could get into the reception area but couldn't get through the doors. The new signage read, 'Bouris, Dowd and Vince'. All hell broke loose. The senior partners called a meeting.

I met with them. I said, 'Well, you realise that we're taking over.'

They said, 'You can't do that, you've got to buy us out.'

'We can't do that.'

'If you take over, you've got to buy us out.'

'No,' I said, 'we're not going to buy you out. I've got no money. I can't pay you.'

They said, 'Well, you have to.'

I said, 'No, I don't. I'm on the lease. I'm a partner, so I'm taking over the premises. I'm taking over the business. You can come in, you can sit in the front, but I've got control of the premises.'

Did I stage a coup? What I said was, 'It's not your business, because the business is the clients and the clients are coming with me. I service the clients.'

I could see they were thinking, *Can he do this?*

Pre-empting them, I said, 'Of course I can, I've just done it. It's been done. It's too late. It's done.'

They said, 'No, no, no, no.'

Anyway, it went on for some months' negotiating and we did become Bouris, Dowd and Vince. We paid them a little bit of money, not much, but we told them they could take all the computer programming they were doing and the Prime Computing client. They could take all that with them. I said, 'Because, to be honest with you, you're doing all the work on that. While we own part of that business too, you can have that. We'll have the accounting practice. You have all of that computing stuff, and we'll pay you a little bit of money.'

They left and went out on their own.

There's an instructional side story to this in terms of making mistakes and being rash and being intellectually arrogant, which I was at that time. Just for a short period of my life, I was very intellectually arrogant.

Here's where my intellectual arrogance got me. That Prime Computing client and the work they were developing went on to become the world's largest online share registry company; it's called Computershare. Of those senior partners, at least one is a very rich person, off the back of Computershare.

At the time their computer work had absolutely no relevance to my life. I didn't know what they were doing. They weren't sharing it with us, either. We were funding their work on that, but they never told us what they were doing.

I thought I could take the firm over and I was driven by the fact that I felt like I was being unfairly treated. But

I learned from that lesson. Everything I've done in my life since, I've never been intellectually arrogant.

I should have gone to them and I should've been more respectful and said, 'Look, I'm not happy with my arrangement here.' Not stage a coup. Intellectually arrogant and naive worked this time but I learned from it.

'There were no mentors, no Svengalis.
I didn't know anybody like that ... yet.'

•

I'm very quick quantitatively. I can calculate things quickly. I'm very good mathematically and I'm very interested in mathematics still. I'm currently reading a book on Indian mathematical systems, going back to ancient India. It's called *Vedic Mathematics* and it's about how 300 years ago they used to calculate things using a different methodology from what we use in the western world. They'd come up with the same answer much faster. Indian kids learn it at school today. That's why they're much better mathematically than our kids are. They're faster. They're faster at doing the boring small bits. That gives them the opportunity to understand the problem and actually work out the proper solutions. I really enjoy understanding patterns, remembering patterns and applying patterns.

I have a deep interest in mathematical sequences, arithmetic sequences, geometric sequences and how formulas and algorithms work, in a mathematical sense. The reason I was good at mathematics at school was because I could remember the formulas and I knew how they fit in terms of patterns. I'm good at that and I have a genuine love of and interest in this field.

For my birthday recently, I was given a book about Euclid. Euclid was a great mathematician. This book was written 200 years ago and it's about Euclid's seven axioms, his mathematical accepted truths about geometry. It's hard going because it was written by someone 200 years ago. It's in English, but the prose is complicated.

I think patterns are important to understand and I apply patterns to people. I might see something in a person that I've seen before, somewhere else, and I'll immediately place that person into that position, which allows me to maybe work out where they're going to end up or what they're like. It's like a particular deduction as a result of all the inputs.

Some people think I'm really instinctive. I actually am not. So why am I good at what I do? I'm good at picking markets which is why, when I did my master's degree, it was in capital markets. Capital markets are all about patterns, like business patterns. Patterns about assets.

Capital markets are about the trading of assets. Not assets as we normally know them but assets like futures or interest rates or mortgages, things like that. They're assets, and they're all priced and they have certain volumes, and there's a whole lot of other things that are associated with them.

My business, Wizard, was never about Wizard the brand, although people thought it was. It was about distribution. In other words, it was how I built a distribution business, how I worked out how to eliminate things that were expensive and put in a variable cost so I could distribute a product. That was also how I manufactured the product. I built a financial technology that allowed me to get money from the capital markets, as they existed then, at the same price the Commonwealth Bank would. And because I had low overheads, I could lend the money at less than the Commonwealth Bank and make more per loan, which made my business very attractive to an investor.

Everyone thinks, 'Oh, you sell on television, you've got a brand.' I didn't do any of that. That was all done by someone else in my business. I sit at the back. They put me in the front because I look a certain way.

They stick me out in the front and say, 'Here, go and do this,' because I can perform. But that's not my real thing. The thing that I really do is the stuff in the back. Back in the Wizard days, as in the Wizard of Oz, I actually financially engineered something that was disruptive financial technology. That's why GE bought me and not anybody else, because I had this engine at the back that no one else had. I could get money. I wouldn't be able to do it today because the world's changed due to the GFC. Back then, I could raise a billion dollars, which I did every six weeks, to lend. I'd go around the world and in front of me would be St George Bank, behind me would be the Commonwealth Bank, ANZ and Westpac. We'd all line up and we'd all go in to see the investors and I'd be trying to get a hundred million dollars out of this investor to fill up a pool of a billion.

They would listen to me the same as they would listen to the Commonwealth Bank and everybody else and I would get my money at least at the same time or before them. The reason why that was the case was because I knew that they were looking for more diversity. Every dollar that I raised wasn't coming out of a Commonwealth Bank branch. It was coming out of my branches plus other people's programs that I funded them with. I had what they call diversity. I had geographical and demographic diversity, so that reduced the risk. I actually had an advantage over the Commonwealth Bank. I got my money before, which meant, if I could always get my money, if liquidity was always available to me and it was available at the right price or an equivalent price, then, given my low overheads, I could always beat them to the gate. Because these were no designer dollars. I'd lend you my dollar at 5 per cent, while the Commonwealth Bank would lend it to you at 5.25 per cent. You'd take my money every day of the week, assuming one thing – that I was credible. I bought my credibility because I gave Kerry Packer half my business, which I'll talk more about later.

That was what I built. That's the pattern that I built. It's just a pattern. It took years of study, studying all the patterns of the capital markets. And I think it's fair to say I got this ability from my mum.

My mum knew everything when it came to opera, music and ballet, she knew everything because she read everything. She went to everything. My Christmas present to my mum and dad, every year, was tickets to the ballet. Every year, maybe for thirty years. She would go to *Swan Lake* every second year because she wanted to see who was new and who was the lead ballerina or who the male lead was, and who was doing the choreography and what was their different interpretation. She could tell you who the best ballerina in Australia was at any given moment and which ballet company she was from. She knew the patterns of ballet. She'd get the programs, and she'd study them and study them and study them so I think I got that trait of analysing patterns from her.

High art bores the shit out of me, but thank God it didn't bore my mother because in the same way that she was interested in it, so I found my love of mathematics and patterns.

I'm big on understanding data and analysing the marketplace. It's curious, but peers and colleagues of mine don't think that way. Some just spray everything and try to get ten hits out of every ninety. Me, I've got to get ten out of ten. It's an obsession for me. It's why I'm still reading books on mathematics – like Euclid – because I like to understand. If you wanted to have a conversation with me about Ayurvedic mathematics one day, not that anyone I've met does, I'd happily converse with you about it.

That obsession is from my mum. That's how she lived her life. And my mum always knew who she was and what mattered to her. I've come a long way since those early days at uni. I can look back and see how I lost myself for a while. But the key to success is knowing who you are, knowing your own strengths and weaknesses and working hard to maximise those positives and minimise the negatives. And admitting when things are getting away from you and doing something about them. Never ever bullshit yourself.

CUT THROUGH YOUR OWN BULLSHIT

1. As hard as it can be, don't allow yourself to be hindered by where you grew up or the socioeconomic bracket you were born into.
2. Clothes shouldn't matter – but they do. So if you are self-conscious or unsure, find what suits you and stick with it.
3. Focus on what's in front of you right now. There's no point worrying about what hasn't yet happened.
4. If you're going to complain, be willing to do something to make a change. No whining.
5. Don't let arrogance put yourself above others. If you do, it will cost you in some way.

ROUND FIVE

Telling It Like It Is

You remember at the start of this book I said that my advice won't always be nice? Well, we're about to get into the not-nice bit. If you want 'nice' then skip this chapter.

The mindset you need

People might be forgiven for thinking that I don't like authority. That's not true. What I don't like is authority for authority's sake. I don't like kings riding through the town with an entourage and me having to kneel and bow my head. No, I don't see the point in that. Why? I don't understand it. I don't see the logic in it. I mean, sure, I'm happy to be respectful but I'm not going to go the next step and bow to the ground. I'm not going to kneel before anybody. Now, whether that's being noncompliant or anti-authoritarian, I don't know. It's just the way I am.

'I've niched myself in this one area,
trying to push the army of small business
warriors into a position of influence.'

I want to show people that you can make your life better. And the definition of 'better' is different for every person. It might not mean making more money, it might mean just having less stress or having an extra half day off each week to spend with your family or to do something you want to do. If you can free yourself up that extra half day can be used in whatever way you choose. You might be able to spend extra time on your business and become more profitable. Or you might be able to study, exercise more, set aside time for divergent thinking or spend time with people who are important to you. You might want to volunteer to do something within your community or you might just want to stare at the sky. Defining your 'better' will mean you can decide how to spend your time.

•

Remember how I told you about the delicatessen/café owner near me who said he was tired from the long hours and he wasn't making that much money? And I said, 'Yeah, but you do something really admirable. People love coming to your shop, you're actually building a community. Not many people get the opportunity to do that. I understand if you don't want to do it anymore. But maybe you need a holiday before you make that decision. Either way, you'll leave a legacy here.' And it's a big deal, I think, contributing to a sense of community. People have a happier life because they are connected. One of the daily highlights for many in my suburb is going to get our coffee first thing in the morning and going back later in the day. It sounds ridiculous, some of these people could be multimillionaires, right? But they're not going to sit inside a closed room and count their money all day long. They don't do that. Life's not like a *Richie Rich* comic. Their highlight is feeling connected to other people, being able to go to their local café and get a cup of coffee and say, 'Hi. How are you going? How're things?'

That's what I'm trying to get small business owners to understand. It is all about hard work and connection.

'It's all up to you. Even with the best people around you, your success or failure is up to you. You can't blame anybody else for what doesn't happen.'

A good example: when the royal commission into banking was going to make recommendations to my industry, I could have sat back and started whingeing, but I didn't. I had to go and do something about it. I mean, if I sat back and just complained and whinged nothing would have happened. Nothing. The government would've gone, 'Oh, okay. Whatever, here's the recommendation. We'll just get on with it.' I had to fight for what I believed in and what I thought was fair and make change possible. That required a lot of hard work.

I had to go and do all those things I promised my shareholders: that I would sell the business, reshape the business and generate my own mortgage product. I couldn't just say it and hope someone else would do it. I had to lead that process and lead it every single day. That's all I thought about through the whole period. And now I am really proud that we've recently launched our mortgage product – it's taken focus, commitment and time but it is worth it to me.

> 'I'm only going to get out of my business what I put
> into it, and I've got to put into it what it requires.'

Work–life balance

The business and the promises you make about your business will determine how many hours you have to work or what you have to do. People talk to me about work–life balance. I think it is important to get it right for yourself but there are times when the balance goes all the work way. If you are serious about your business then you choose to do this without fighting it because you want to succeed. Sometimes you have to look at the long game and put the effort in to make things better down the track. So you really need to ask the tough questions of yourself before you attempt to build a business or take on the role of entrepreneur. You have to be honest with yourself and realise nothing is ever given to you, you have to work at it. Answer these seven questions.

1. Do you want to be in business?
2. What is that business?
3. What are the promises you make to the market, your market?
4. What are the promises you make to your staff?
5. What are the promises you make to yourself?
6. What are the problems you face?
7. What does it take to fulfil all this?

The answers to these questions will determine how many hours you work and they will determine your work–life balance.

You don't like that? Then you aren't ready and you are setting yourself up to fail. Don't make the promises. Don't be in that industry. Don't be an innovator or an entrepreneur. There is no shame in working for a wage if that is what you want. But don't bullshit yourself that you are an entrepreneur if you are only half-hearted about anything. Go and find something else. Work–life balance is about doing things you've promised to do and putting in the hours to achieve the things you promised to do, or that the marketplace you're in requires you to do. Small business is not for the faint-hearted. If you don't like it, it's not the marketplace's problem, it's your problem, so leave. Go do something else. Go work for somebody where you can go to work, do your job and come home at night, sit down and watch Netflix.

This is my approach to business. The goal is to be provocative, controversial even, but never offensive. But be honest with yourself. Do you really want it? And if you do, go for it.

'Don't be afraid of infamy.'

Infamy depends on who the audience is. In business, sometimes infamy means that there are people who don't like what you say, or it doesn't fit with their ethics. John

Symond of Aussie Home Loans once said, 'The banks are arseholes.' The big banks thought he was infamous because he didn't promote their cause, but what he was doing was promoting the cause of consumers. That's an example of infamy.

It depends on who the listener is as to whether you're famous or infamous, based on their ethics in relation to business, and their ethics in relation to what you're saying. But if you are true to yourself, don't hurt anyone and don't break the law then be proactive, speak out against a status quo you think is wrong and stand up for yourself no matter what.

Don't be afraid to be unpopular

I take the view if 50 per cent of people like you and 50 per cent of people hate you, then at least you've got 50 per cent. If you try and please everybody you get no one. And you won't be heard. You'll never please everyone.

Don't question yourself out of an idea

I never say to myself, *That's a dumb idea. I'll pass that one by.* I never think like that. With divergent thinking you can look at all options and work things out before problems arise. To do that you have to look at all possibilities. Generally speaking, before I act I've already explored my options and run through possible outcomes. I get one or two good ideas and I run with them until I exhaust them. It's the only way to go. I don't sit and question myself around the idea until I get to the point where I've sanitised it so much that the idea's gone; it's disappeared up its own arse.

The world is littered with people who say, 'I had this idea once.' And you feel like saying, 'Why didn't you act on it? That was a great idea.'

Of course, this all has a relationship, probably an inverse relationship, to what you do day-to-day to earn money. If you work as an electrician and it pays your bills, but you have another idea and you ask me, 'Mark, what should I do?' I'd say to you, 'Well, continue your day job, work on the other one as a side hustle or an idea hustle.' Like we talked about earlier. 'Build it up to the point where you can flip the two over, but your idea has got to be demonstrating enough success before it can be flipped to the first position and then your electrician job can be put to bed.' While you're testing the idea's commercial potential you shouldn't get rid of your day-to-day job. You should always attend to what's putting bread on the table.

Keep tending the garden

I'm paraphrasing one of my favourite films here, *Being There*. To anyone who's in business at the moment, I would say, 'Watch *Being There*.'

It's a cerebral film. It's about simplicity. Peter Sellers plays a simpleton or maybe he's not such a simpleton after all? I won't spoil your fun by telling you what happens, but the central theme of the film is that 'Life is a state of mind'.

I think that's really apt at the moment. If you want your life to be better you've got to change your state of mind. Challenge things, don't listen to what everybody else tells you. And I'd say to you, don't believe everything everyone's telling you. You can control your state of mind. You can feel as good as your perspective allows you. Think positively. Some people say, 'think abundantly', or maybe just think simply before everything becomes abundant.

The main character of *Being There*, Chance the gardener (Peter Sellers), is a great example of thinking simply. I like the message of the film, that thinking simply allows you to think more clearly. A cluttered mind hinders clarity. When you think simply you have a clear vision of what's going on. Instead of thinking, *Is this a recession or a depression?* – think of this as the winter.

Winter's actually good. What do plants do in the winter? They grow roots under the ground and they get ready for the spring. Okay, so that's your cue to get ready for the spring. Do the prep now because sooner or later things are going to turn around. Everything goes through cycles – business, property, moods, life – so learn to adjust yourself to those cycles and manage them by managing your state of mind. And with that focus you can ask yourself questions and the answers will lead your actions.

What can I do? Where is there demand? Where does it look like opportunities will pop up? Because there will be opportunities even in hard times. You might say to yourself, *I don't have a job – should I be doing a course to improve my skills? Should I just go and work anywhere? Should I do something no one else wants to do – be a labourer, drive a courier van? If I drive a courier van then maybe I'll get to understand the courier game really well, maybe I'll be able to buy my own courier van, then maybe two. One day I might have a fleet of courier vans?*

You have to make things happen for yourself, no one is going to do it for you. So if you don't have a job or are only working two days a week or whatever the case may be don't think you can't make things better. You can choose to work really hard on yourself, become better at something. Direct yourself to become better at things that are going to get you something in the future. I'm not talking about becoming a scientist necessarily – although maybe that is the answer for some people – but becoming a courier is a great example. It means just driving a van, delivering whatever. But you can start to understand how warehouses work logistically; how does a warehouse work relative to the courier who delivers? What do people want from a courier? What does a consumer want from a courier? What do they want from me? Then start expanding your thinking around that. That's what I mean by life is a state of mind.

Think about nature. Everything we do is the same as nature. We don't do anything different. That's why I love *Being There*. As I write this book people are talking about us being in recession. So think of this as the winter. I've nothing going on up top so I'm going to put all my effort down below.

It's all about looking after the garden. At the end of the winter, when all of the leaves have fallen off and there's no fruit, then you start looking at what's going on below the soil. You looked after the roots because you knew that the spring would come again. You must always tend the garden no matter what. You need to take that knowledge and transplant it to yourself so you can make things change. Don't waste energy on whingeing or pointing blame. Get on with it.

'Life is a state of mind. And your state of mind
is: I'm going to continue on with this business.
I'm not going to whinge and carry on about it.'

Don't ever settle for how things are if you aren't happy or
want more from your life. There was a line I heard once in
a movie that stuck with me, 'You get what you settle for'.
Don't settle. Start looking for possibilities, then fire up
and build that possibility on the side of your regular life.
Build it slowly and carefully. Focus your state of mind on
making things better. I can't stress strongly enough the
idea that you must never ever resile from the position that
you must continue doing the things that actually keep the
fires burning for you. Never lose sight of the fact that you
work hard to make your life better.

The fire can never go out

If you've found some other way to make a bigger fire don't
let the fact that you've got to do it after work discourage
you. If you are discouraged or resentful or angry that you
are working longer and harder or studying so much then
it can't be that good an idea or you can't be that excited
about it.

You can't complain about the fact that you have to
work nine to five or you're working eight hours a day

115

stoking the fire just to survive. None of this, 'It's not fair.' That's all bullshit. You've got to put the effort in. If that means working harder for longer to be productive for yourself you have to do it. And if you've got an idea, be patient, be prepared to take time. If you're worried that someone else is going to knock off the idea before you can make it your own then maybe you need to consider going about it in a different way. For example, maybe you need to have a partner to help you. You might need more resources or skills or money.

I wouldn't suggest always putting your own money into a new possibility. You don't have to let that limit you. You can find someone who believes in what you're saying and get them to partner with you. But it's no one's responsibility except yours. And your life is your life. You've got to make sure you continue to tend your garden. You've taken a long time to build that garden, you've got to keep tending it. Because the moment you start forgetting the gardening and go elsewhere and neglect it, the garden will overgrow and you're fucked. The roots will be no good, things will start dying.

What is backing yourself?

Backing yourself means you're working every night and every day. That's just what it takes. I think the gene for hard work is in the DNA of any person who wants to be their own businessman or woman and makes it happen. And you have to be brave. You have to be willing to back yourself even when others might think your idea is the craziest idea on the planet. New ideas, crazy ideas, these are what make new businesses fly. Think of Bill Gates working in a garage or, close to home, Karin Adcock, who introduced Pandora jewellery to the Australian market and created a trend and made money in the process.

The sound businessperson incubates or greenhouses the idea while looking after their garden. You've got your garden, and then you've got your room over here where you've got your seeds. And you're trying to discover a new variety of pear. You're working on that every night, pulling the seed out, looking at it, and examining it, and trying to propagate it, etc. But no matter what happens you don't walk away from that garden. You do your research at night. Even if it means you're there burning the lamp until late. But you're still going to get up tomorrow morning when the sun rises and tend to your garden. That's what I'm talking about as a state of mind. Your state of mind has to be: *That's what I'm doing, that's how I'm going to go about it, that's my plan. I'll revisit this in twelve months' time.*

That's what I would say to people in business who have a great idea. Great, prosecute that idea, but build it slowly. You've got to be very careful with these things, you do have to pull the seed out, and you have to wait until it's ready to grow.

At the moment I've actually been growing rocket, but the rocket's gone to seed now. I can't just go and pull seeds out, I have to wait until everything opens up, and it's ready for me to take the seeds out. I'll go around and I'll pick all the seeds up and I'll put them in a little packet. And then I'll put the packet in a bag and then I'll put them somewhere until the time and conditions are right and then I'll replant those rocket seeds. The particular rocket I'm growing is a big broad-leaf rocket, it's called salad rocket. Salad rocket is hard to get. It's like arugula. The traditional peppery rocket. Really big, thick leaves on it. So you don't have to pick a whole lot of little ones.

At home, my dad's got lettuce. My dad knows how to do this stuff. He's got lettuce leaf seeds, shitloads of them. He grows lettuces and most vegetables just from the seeds he's collected over the years. They're organic. He knows what to expect when he grows them. He knows what particular types of vegetables he likes. And the shape, the taste. It's a very slow process but the end result is worth it. The end result is abundance of what my dad wants.

People who say, 'I'm going to get up and leave everything, and I'm going to go and do that.' Well, that's a big risk. Because you need money. You've got to pay your rent. It's different if you're some youngster with no obligations. But, generally speaking, most of the ideas come from people who aren't that young.

•

When the money's on the table, take the money

I'm not a gambler. No way. If I'm winning, I'll take the money off the table. I'm not going to say I'll reinvest it. I won't say I'll have another bet with what I've just won.

I start businesses, and build businesses, and make them valuable, hopefully. It doesn't always work like that. But if someone offers you $100,000 for your business and you think it's around the money, don't hang out for $105,000. The $100,000, that's the money. I don't want this to be misinterpreted. I'd take the $100,000. I'd take it off the table. I don't leave any money on the table, I take it, that's a hundred grand. People always think, *Shit, I could have got more for that*. I never walk away thinking I could have got more.

119

I got what I got. It's okay. Take what you got and go start again, do something else. Don't sit there thinking, *I could have got more money.*

Don't fuck around. Kerry Packer told me that. I did a deal with General Electric to sell Wizard – which I'll go into in detail later – and the ANZ bank was interested in buying us for more money. Kerry said to me, 'Son, you do what you think is the right thing.' And I took GE's money. It was more likely to occur even though it was a lesser amount. They'd done all the work, they were ready to go, ANZ wasn't.

Being bold doesn't mean being stupid

This whole kind of conservative, non-risk-taking, not gambling, tending to the garden, making sure the fire's burning, taking what's on the table – this is probably contrary to what people who don't know me might think I'm about.

I know some probably think, *Wow, he's a maverick, challenging the status quo,* and in many ways I am. But that doesn't mean I take stupid risks or am prepared to burn my hard work for slightly more gain. What I'm counselling for is a very concerted approach. Yes, you've got to challenge on the one hand, you've got to question the status quo. Don't go along with things just because everyone says, 'This is the way it's been done, that's how we should do it.' For me, risk is about doing the research, knowing the market, knowing your own strengths and knowing what others are on about. You calculate what some might see as risk and then be bold enough to dig deeper. And you don't get greedy.

'That's where I take the risk. I push back
and question the status quo.'

Entrepreneurs are not mavericks

I follow a very tight, logical, purposeful process. The old-style entrepreneur took huge risks, I don't take risks like that. It's a crazy idea – a shoot from the hip kinda thing.

That's not how I go about it. You can't do it today. You might've been able to do it ten, twenty years ago, but today there's too much shit in the way. You have to go about things in a logical process. Machine learning.

People come to me looking for silver bullet solutions. I don't have them. I can show you the disciplines you've got to follow to get results, but I can't do it for you. That's what the mentor thing is all about. It's not about me giving you an answer. It is about me showing you the skills you need to develop to find the answers yourself.

I can only ask you the questions. Are you prepared to do this? Can you do this? What about this? What about that? Then you've got to come up with the answers. The answers lay within you. I don't have the answers to how to run a delicatessen or an engineering shop or whatever. I can't run a panel beater's shop, I can't do it, I wouldn't have a clue. But I know how to encourage someone to lay the foundations so they can do any of those things if that is where their possibility lies. So mentoring is about questioning. What are you doing? How are you going? How's the money going?

The key thing is to know what your purpose is, which we'll come to later. Once you can get clarity on that, then there'll be clarity in your message.

We all get periods where we don't know how to do something. You think, *Fuck, how am I going to get through this GST period? How am I going to negotiate with the bank going forward? How am I going to increase my revenue?*

'When you can't work out the answer to how, you can get quite down, you can get very stressed out and anxious. Only one thing will save you: remembering *why.*'

The business owners of Australia have been going through the most dreadful situations recently – bushfires, drought, COVID-19 lockdowns – and most are still trying to work out how to survive. Whenever you face any adversity in business, remembering what your purpose is can actually help save you because the 'how' will come about sooner or later. But while you're waiting, you're going to live a life of anxiety if you don't have a why. Why do you want this?

If you don't know why you're in business, and what your purpose is, then you should. The how – when it comes, because it always does – is about dealing with things you don't have control of. The why part – you've got control of that. That's your choice. You choose to have that purpose. The purpose is in front of you, it's written down. If you haven't written it down, you should. You choose that.

Viktor Frankl was an Austrian neurologist and Holocaust survivor. Over a nine-day period he wrote an unbelievable book called *Man's Search for Meaning* based on his experience in various Nazi concentration camps. Can you imagine being someone like Viktor Frankl? How he survived? He remembered what was important to him and despite the odds, he got through. I am not saying everything will be okay if you know your purpose because life can be cruel and things completely outside your control can impact hard and change everything. But if you know your purpose you have a focus and you can hold on to that and to hope and possibility. That can be a way through to better times.

IT IS ALL UP TO YOU

1. Mindset is everything. Don't let negativity defeat you before you start.
2. Blame no one but yourself – success or failure is up to you.
3. Know what you want in work and in life. Don't kid yourself if you're half-hearted about being an entrepreneur.
4. Have faith in your ideas – new, crazy, innovative ideas are what make businesses fly.

Contender

As a young man I learned a lot fast but I look back and think I could have learned a lot more if I hadn't been so quick to discount the experience of the older partners. If there had been a mentoring program, like the one I've developed recently, it might have helped lessen the divide between the established members of the firm and those looking to make their mark. But there wasn't anything like that then. After the coup I stayed in the accounting firm for one more year but I became bored and moved on to the law firm we worked with, Symonds and Baffsky. Bouris, Dowd and Vince paid me a royalty for the use of my name for four or five years after I left the accounting firm, which still exists today but it's called Einfeld Symonds Vince (ESV).

Market on the run

Symonds and Baffsky was a well-established, well-known, highly respected law firm in Sydney. It was the 1980s and it was an unbelievable time to be in business. I learned my craft in the 1980s and was able to experience a lot.

There were a lot of scallywags around, but people were also more free in their thinking. In my opinion, people were much more creative and less worried about the consequences. And, to be frank, they bent the rules a lot, but they bent them in a creative sense.

So it was an interesting time to watch others and observe how they went about things. Alan Bond was one of our clients, we had a lot of clients like him. They were hardworking, big thinkers, extremely creative and pushing the boundaries. People who tried to make things happen, who were fearless, but then there were those who pushed things too far, became reckless and crossed the line. For a young bloke like me, watching and learning, it was really interesting.

We also had a lot of smart people in our firm and, again, as a young guy I could watch, observe and learn from them. So not only did I have the opportunity to be around clients who were really creative and smart, and intellectually aggressive, I also had lots of good people at the firm to learn from. People who were open to mentoring. It was a great baseline to jump off from.

The senior partner at the firm – David Baffsky – was a wonderful businessperson. He didn't necessarily teach me, it wasn't like that, but he would question me and push me to find my own answers. He was unbelievably brilliant at giving me the opportunity to do things my way, and he would back my ability. He allowed me to experiment. It was like a scientist being told, 'Look, you're allowed this sort of stuff, go for it.'

My main role in the firm was to fully understand the laws around banking and structured finance. An example was if we had a client who wanted to buy something worth a lot of money in those days, like a $10 million knitting mill from the Netherlands or something, there had to be finance involved. A lot of times, an acquisition mightn't make financial sense in terms of interest that had to be paid or the price that was being asked considering you were working with Australian volumes unless you could do what they call a structured deal. Then you could somehow make it tax effective for both the buyer (or lease holder) and the investor or finance company, which might not even operate in Australia. They used to have things in those days called double-dips, where you dipped twice into the tax treaties. You had to structure a deal so it was watertight. I don't mean from a tax point of view but watertight from a commercial viewpoint.

The lessor was happy, the lessee – who was our client – was happy, the tax office was happy. The ruling was in favour of everybody. The vendor, in the case of the knitting mill example, who was selling the machine to the lessor, they were happy. There might have been five or six parties and complicated deals, big deals which might've involved four or five countries. It was a really interesting time and for a 28-year-old guy it was pretty cool stuff to be doing. So that was my role in the firm. I was one of the main people in that area. I did that for about five, six years.

After that, the firm changed and a lot of the things that we had been doing were legislated out. The Australian government said, 'We don't like this, we're going to change that legislation so you can't do it anymore.' The firm changed its name, a lot of people left, some went on to other firms. My brother had been there working with me and he moved to another firm at this time. The senior partner and I moved into property work. We started doing well. He became involved with a listed property company in Australia, which he sort of controlled, and I continued with him and became involved in building hotels and businesses like that.

Between the ages of thirty and forty, I tried lots of different things. I went through some tough periods of not feeling as though I had any purpose in life. This was when I had moved from a proper structure with the law firm – we had to fill the timesheets, do billing, collect the money, see the clients, keep records, and the like – to working in property, which was a totally different environment. In the law firm, everything was accountable. Every six minutes I spent was accountable. If you're my client, I give you advice, I write down the advice I've given you, I send you a letter with the advice recorded over the six minutes I spent with you. Then, at the end of the month, I get my work-in-progress and I bill you, then I chase you up. It was structured and straightforward. Whereas in the property business it's different.

To me, property is a lot more extemporaneous. You're out looking for property, you're talking to engineers, you're talking to architects, you look at this deal, it might be the right deal for you; or this other deal might be better. You eventually find one you hone in on. Then you're trying to get it funded by the banks, and then you've got to get it built and constructed. I'm not an engineer. I'm not a builder. I'm not the architect. It was more about delegating jobs to others to work on your behalf. You've got to sort out contracts – we used lawyers. In the past, I was always on that side, being given things to sort out for someone else. Now I was handing stuff out to people and having to wait for them to deliver. It was very different, and for a period there, it was like my first six months of university; I was a bit lost again.

I was in another relationship at that stage with a woman who would become my second wife. I had one child who lived overseas with his mother. They had agreed to come back to Australia. My son was five and he was coming back from France to start school in Australia. I hadn't seen him for three or four years though I used to ring him all the time. Communication was difficult because I wasn't in a position to just fly over to Europe whenever I wanted to, so the distance meant I was missing out on spending time with my son, and he was missing out on knowing his dad. That was something I had to deal with and it also factored in to me feeling a bit lost.

When I got married again, my wife got pregnant not long after. I had another kid on the way and my son was moving back to Australia, so my responsibilities were starting to jack up a bit. I needed to make sure that I had enough income to support everybody. That was important to me.

I wasn't making a shitload of money, but I was making enough. I was dabbling in things, trying different things.

During that period, I bought into a modest mortgage business. I had been watching other new players in the industry, like Rams and Aussie (Aussie Home Loans). I didn't really know Rams, but I knew Aussie's owner John Symond quite well. I was watching the impact they were having on the industry and I thought, *I reckon I can do that.* I thought I could do the same thing, but I thought I could do it a different way, and hopefully a bit better.

I had the academic experience and qualifications in that area. I understood what was going on, and I was always researching, so I felt confident that I could take the business that existed, the little broking business that I'd bought into, and make it something more. I was going to change its name and I was confident that I could take on Aussie and Rams. When I think back now, it was quite bold, but somehow I did it.

It took me a little bit of time to get my team together and get my feet on the ground. I had the business knowledge and I knew the law and how lending worked. But there was one thing I didn't know. And I was about to take a crash course.

'I had to understand marketing. I'd never marketed anything in my life. I had to work out how to do it.'

John Symond at Aussie was fantastic at what he was doing and he had the backing of Macquarie Bank. I didn't have the backing of anybody at that stage. But I was pretty fearless at the time and to be honest, to some extent, a lot of it was born out of naivety. If I had known then what I know now, I might not have done any of the things I did. But they worked, I was blessed that they worked. Some of those things wouldn't work now, but the times were right for them to work out for me and the business.

The business was called Mortgage Acceptance Corporation. It was made up of four brokers. If you were a borrower, if you wanted to borrow money, you went and saw a broker and, in those days, the broker charged you. The bank didn't pay the broker, you did. These brokers would say, if you're going to borrow $100,000, we'll charge you 1 per cent, which is a thousand bucks. They'd find out which bank had an appetite for your credit. It was a lot easier in those days than it is today and these four were good at their job. In fact, the reason I'd met them was because I was doing a development down in the Southern Highlands with one of my business partners. We'd bought an old school site, and we had twelve months to settle. In those days, in the country, you would get funding from the Rural

Bank, which was a bank that funded country people. Between exchange and settlement on this development, the Rural Bank changed its name to the State Bank of New South Wales and put its head office in Sydney. With that move it decided it only wanted to lend to 'normal' lending projects. All of a sudden our specialist lender disappeared and changed the goalposts. As the months ticked by and the settlement date for the project loomed, the source of funding we had thought was a done deal evaporated. And I had no success in finding it elsewhere. We had to find the money, and we had to find it quickly. One of the women who worked in our development office had a friend who was a broker and she suggested, 'Why don't you go see this guy?'

I'd never dealt with a mortgage broker before and, at that point, I would have dealt with Satan himself just to get the loan approved. Within three or four days, that broker did get a loan approved. It was crazy. I'd been trying for months and I couldn't get it done myself. He got it approved in three or four days with the Commonwealth Bank. I thought it was interesting that he could do this stuff so well.

So I met all these partners and said, 'Look, let's have a talk. Do you know Aussie Home Loans and Rams? I reckon you can do the same thing as them.'

And they said, 'Rubbish.'

I said, 'No, you could.'

I had lunch with them at a place called Stuyvesant's House on Sydney's north shore because their office was upstairs. I said, 'You can for sure.' And I told them I'd invest in them. I didn't have much money, but I sold my house and invested some money into their business. And I said, 'We've got to change the name, you've got to become retail.' So, I needed to come up with a name.

What's in a name? Everything!

I had a reason for coming up with a new name. I'd done a lot of reading about Virgin. I always thought Virgin was a great marketing business, by which I mean, great at marketing themselves. And I remember studying the name, thinking, *Why does the name work?* Apart from it being controversial, it's a name you remember because it has some strong sounding letters like I, R, G, I, N. 'VIR' – it's a strong sound. It has aural impact.

I decided I had to come up with a word that had strong sounding letters and made an impact when you heard it spoken but that also had some relevance. I had twenty different candidates and, as I looked through them, I thought that one was all right: Wizard. I could play around with it, but I also liked the sound of 'ARD',

Wiz-ard. It's a word that has an effect on you, like Virgin. It was a bit controversial because, in the banking sector, Aussie was already a different name for that industry. To call yourself Aussie Home Loans was different because everyone else had institutional names like Westpac, Australia and New Zealand Banking Group – really conservative, straight down the line. Aussie had kept a patriotic theme going and I was going to completely mix it all up. I thought, because it's Wizard, people would think, *What the fuck?*

People think I chose Wizard because of *The Wizard of Oz*. That wasn't the case, that was something that came later. I picked Wizard because I thought of financial wizardry, sayings like 'she's a financial wizard'. I also thought it was a name we could play with because a lot of sportspeople are called wizards on the field. There was a guy playing AFL – Jeff Farmer of Fremantle – who was called 'the wizard' and there was a Rugby League player for the Roosters, Gary Freeman, who was called 'the wiz'. Sporting connotations and financial wizardry were a good combination. But, ultimately, I just thought it was a good name. At the end of the day, I remembered Richard Branson writing somewhere that he didn't really care if people liked the name Virgin or not.

'As long as people remember the name, and you deliver on it, you deliver something they like – they *like* you. Not because of the name, they like you because of what you do for them. They remember you because of the name.'

Made sense to me. I thought I'd get a name, then I'd give great service. That's all that was going through my head. And I knew these four brokers would give good service, because they were *really* good. I found them likeable, efficient, they knew the marketplace and they were fast, hungry and young, they were all around thirty.

When I shared the name, one of the brokers didn't particularly like it. He'd come up with the company's original name, so he didn't want it to be changed. At that point I had 40 per cent of the business, and him and another broker had quite big percentages and then the other two brokers, who were really young, only had very small percentages.

But after talking it through we went with Wizard and we got the business up and running. It was going okay. I really had nothing to do with it. I was just an investor, I wasn't even on the board. I thought I would watch and see how it went first because I had a few other things I had to clean up; I had a few property developments on the go that I had to finish up.

Perfecting the art of the skirmish

One of the first things I knew we had to do was advertise. The company didn't have much money, and all the money we had was from selling my house. The others didn't present any money so I don't think they had any to share. We did a few ads in the newspaper. I'd never advertised in my life and we didn't have an advertising agency to help us.

I remember going to – this is 1997 – the *Sunday Telegraph* and I said, 'How much is the inside back page?' The *Sunday Telegraph* was the number one newspaper in those days and the inside back page was a good page to advertise on. They said you can have the whole page for twenty-five grand. I thought, *Shit, I can only actually afford one page.* They gave me the space and they designed it for us, but it wasn't anything special. I spent $25,000 and they got my phone number wrong.

Now it's funny, you know, I was devastated when I opened the paper that Sunday morning. I was furious and I rang them up and said, 'You've damaged my business, you've stuffed me, people are ringing up and they can't get through. It's bad for my reputation and bad for my brand.' I went off my nut. They placated me by giving me two free full back-page ads. I got another $50,000 worth of prime advertising out of it. That worked all right. We got three ads in three weeks, and we got quite a lot of enquiries from them. That was my first foray into advertising or real marketing. I thought, *Well, that's not bad.*

'It's about leveraging stuff.'

After those first three ads I heard that the rugby league State of Origin was coming up in two weeks' time, and Aussie Home Loans was advertising in the second-tier competition, called the Aussie Home Loans Cup (now the NRL Schoolboy Cup), which is like a young person's game. Aussie was a sponsor. They had offered the State of Origin to John Symond too, but he hadn't come back with an answer. The game was coming up and Tooheys, the New South Wales team's sponsor, had pulled out and New South Wales was going into the game without a sponsor, which was bad on so many levels. A friend of mine told me this, and he put me in contact with the CEO of the New South Wales Rugby League.

This was in the middle of the Super League war and a lot of the usual State of Origin players were playing Super League and couldn't play State of Origin. So, no sponsor, some players missing but, still, the game was a spectacle and people wanted to watch it. They asked me if I was interested. I did a deal with them. Someone told me that I pissed off John Symond of Aussie Home Loans because he thought that they should have given it to him because he had been sponsoring the Aussie Home Loans Cup for ages. But he was away and maybe the message didn't get passed on to him that there was an opportunity and in that vacuum I grabbed it. I was there, Johnny-on-the-spot. I gave them a cheque, which was the last money I had out of the sale of my house.

The cheque was for a quarter of a million dollars and I said, 'I'll pay you upfront tomorrow, but I want it for three years.' I told them the amount and that I also wanted seats, tickets, shit like that, promotional things and the name on the jersey. Because there was only a week to go, they didn't have time to put jerseys in the shops, but I did get our name on the players' jerseys. That was a bit of a coup because people were saying, 'Who the hell is Wizard on this jersey?' And it was very prominent. It was good for people to ask the question, 'Who's Wizard?' And for me, that worked.

In 1999, when the Commonwealth Bank decided to float half of the shares in the bank, they decided to reduce the interest rates for mortgages out of cycle. Normally, the convention was that you only reduced interest rates for a mortgage when the Reserve Bank reduced interest rates and you increased interest rates when the Reserve Bank increased interest rates. It was a strictly adhered to convention and pretty much everyone was on the same rate. The Commonwealth Bank reduced interest rates to celebrate and mark their public listing with those shares. Everyone was talking about the fact that it was going to happen. It did happen. The Commonwealth Bank took their rate from 7.1 per cent to 6.99 per cent.

I thought, okay, we're already in securitisation, meaning we already had someone else's platform giving us money to lend to people as a Wizard Home Loan. Our business at that stage was not doing securitisation, but we were getting this money from a securitisation platform, a very famous one at the time, which is now owned by NAB. But it wasn't then, it was privately owned. I remember sitting around with my team; we had done the *Sunday Telegraph* advertising, we were on the State of Origin jersey. I thought, *Now we're going to come up with a product to catch everyone's attention.* And we did. In February 1999, the Commonwealth Bank came out with the 6.99 per cent product, the very next day Wizard offered a deal at 6.98 per cent. Boom!

The newspapers hadn't seen this before, it'd never happened before. The headline in the *Australian Financial Review* was: 'Wizard Leads with Magic Rate.'

Beautiful. That's where the 'magic' thing started to slip into the Wizard promotions, then it started to become

The Wizard. Then I started playing on *The Wizard of Oz* stuff. I encouraged that in the media and they played with it because it suited them.

I am very aware of how things work in the media. In this country they will build you up, but it's not something that lasts. I know they've got to do a job, but they build you up so they can pull you down. They build volatility. They build volatility with personalities and they build volatility with brands. They love instability and destabilisation and will feed it (and even create it) because it gives them a story every time, either on the way up or on the way down. So Wizard comes out with this rate of 6.98 per cent, and it was a leader. It gave me credibility, because the *Australian Financial Review* in those days had credibility, and if they were positive it impacted. People started to notice us and they tied it back to the Wizard on the jersey. We had the State of Origin coming up in May that year, so it wasn't that far away.

Then Channel 9's weeknight TV show *A Current Affair* rang. They wanted to know what was going on. I did one interview on *A Current Affair* and our phones went off. We had a little office in Artarmon, like the smallest office you've ever seen in your life. We couldn't handle the phone calls, it was just crazy. We had 800 phone calls in a day. We probably didn't deal with 600 of them and we realised, *Shit, we're onto something here.* That was before the State of Origin effect took off again.

Those first three years advertising with the State of Origin was brilliant for me. After that it was just maintenance, but the first three years were so good. As always, I learned from watching what others did. I don't know if you remember the ads on the sides of buses when they launched Tommy Hilfiger in Australia. They rented that space, owned it. The name 'Tommy' was just about everywhere for a long time. People were asking, 'Who's this Tommy?' Now I could never have afforded to do that, but I did know people were asking, 'Who's this Wizard?' The fact that they asked the question, and then if you come and tell them who Wizard is – like Tommy Hilfiger did – you can build a brand. Tommy Hilfiger spent shitloads of money doing it and they obviously have an international brand, but, you know, diluted down, that's what I wanted to do.

> 'Self-schooled, self-educated marketing, advertising,
> PR branding, education; creating a brand from the
> ground up – not bad for a boy from Punchbowl!'

I didn't have anybody, I was just making it up. No media qualifications, no marketing degree. It was just me saying, 'Let's try this.'

I made some mistakes, some things didn't work, but nothing significant. But even with things going well, I knew I didn't have enough money to invest to make things bigger. I didn't have enough capital. It was all right for me to sell my house and put money into the State of Origin and all that sort of stuff, but how was I going to keep coming up with the dough? That is when you have to ask all the questions, use divergent thinking and chase the answers you need. So I did.

The mindset of an entrepreneur

As an entrepreneur you have to be a fast mover. An entrepreneur identifies a problem and comes up with a solution. Then you've got to execute it. And the skills they teach at universities are how to execute. Most entrepreneurs don't know how to close the deal in their heads. You have to be bold and back yourself. And you can't think one success is enough. You have to keep nimble and keep coming up with solutions and strategies to maintain a business and even more so to build one up. Most entrepreneurs are more like – there's a problem here's a solution, there I've done it. But that's it, they fail after that. They fuck it up.

This is what this book is about. I learned my business knowledge on the run, but I had general skills from uni and an understanding about a structured organisation from my work at the law firm. I had a good idea of how that works.

•

When I was able to turn the deficit of the *Sunday Telegraph* getting my phone number wrong into more ads, rather than throwing my toys out of the pram, I learned from that experience. I realised this was a way to get more advertisements for the little money I had.

I did it again with Channel 9. The world of television in those days was all about who's making a noise about their brand, who's just kicking off a brand, who's in a competitive environment? This is what TV people do and how they think. Who wants a leg-up with their brand; who will spend a bit of money, throw a bit of money around? They're always scanning for this sort of person. Harvey Norman is a good example. TV sales executives chase Harvey Norman all the time. I knew that. And I thought, well, I've got to be that sort of brand. Doing these little skirmishes, like the State of Origin and the Commonwealth Bank thing, helped. But we needed more.

I knew that someone was going to pick me up on their radar sooner or later and I was right. Channel 9 had a production group who were always scanning the media. They'd have a show and want to build an audience so they'd look at competitions and giveaways. Someone there said, 'We need someone to give ten thousand dollars away on *The Footy Show*,' because *The Footy Show* is always looking for content. What happened? A little regional rugby league clubhouse burnt down and *The Footy Show* wanted to give $10,000 to that club to rebuild. But Channel 9 and *The Footy Show* didn't want to put the money up themselves. Their thinking was, *Let's find someone out there who we think we can talk into doing that.*

Someone in their production team saw me on *A Current Affair* and mentioned it to the group. The executive producer was like, 'Let's ring this guy.' They did and when the opportunity was put to me I jumped on it.

In the meantime, a good mate of mine, David Gyngell, was at Mark McCormack's IMG. And this is a good example of the way these things happened then. Australia was playing against New Zealand in a rugby union test match, and IMG had been asked to find a sponsor the day before the test match. Australia didn't have a jersey sponsor for that game. The game was being played at the Sydney Football Stadium and was going to be televised to the rest of the world. David gives me a ring because we were good mates and he asked, 'Do you want to do it?' And I asked, 'How much?' Well, they wanted ninety grand but we got it down to fifty the night before the game. We got it down, him and me negotiating with them, and IMG probably got a commission. We did the deal at night, and the next day we had the name Wizard spray-painted 3D style on the pitch, had it painted on all the hoardings along the sidelines so that the cameras picked it up. And we were on the jerseys.

For $50,000 my brand was on the TV for ninety minutes. So, I did these little skirmishes, and I did it with help – David was great and negotiated that deal for me. I didn't understand the 3D printing thing on the field; he knew all that stuff. I'll never forget, it was him and me and his secretary. She was typing up the agreement while David and I were sitting in the room together, sending it off to the ARL, and we got the deal done.

But back to *The Footy Show*. I get a phone call from the executive producer. 'Mark, we've got this thing, we want to give ten thousand dollars away, can you come on *The Footy Show*?' I said, 'Yeah okay. No worries, mate.' I get on the show, and Paul 'Fatty' Vautin was the main host then. He was a great footy player with a good footy brain but his on-screen persona was sometimes a little goofy. They asked me to muck around and come out with a suitcase that they made look like it was full of cash; it wasn't. I had to give the money away and Fatty introduces me as 'Michael Bouris'. He got that wrong and they didn't say the name of Wizard Home Loans. I was livid.

I rang the executive producer the next day. I fucking went to town, and I said, 'You know, that's not what I signed up for and blah, blah, blah.' He said, 'Look, don't worry. We'll give you a mention next week.' It was like the *Sunday Telegraph* thing all over again. 'We'll get Fatty to get on there and say he got your name wrong,' and everything like that. I said, 'Okay.' The following Thursday, I'm sitting at home, I'll never forget. I was watching *The Footy Show*, waiting for this segment to come on, which it did. Fatty says, 'Last week, we had a really generous donation from this guy. I called him Michael Bouris, his name is Mark Bouris,' and he then continues on, saying, 'he's one of those thingummyjigs'. He fucked it up again. I know it was part of his schtick on the show but it made me the joke and I wasn't happy. 'And it's called Wizard Home Loans,' and they just laughed it off. And that was it. I was straight on the phone to the executive producer, saying, 'Mate, that's no fucking good. That is fucked. You know, "a thingummyjig", you're joking with me, like, that's worse.' The producer said, 'Don't worry. We'll get you up again.' I got three weeks' worth of three-minute promotions. The next week, the third week, was beautiful. The Chief (Paul Harragon, ex-Kangaroo and captain of the Newcastle Knights) took the promotion on this time, and he nailed it: he thanked me – Mark Bouris, he thanked Wizard Home Loans, 'They give you home loans, they look after your loan for you, they're a mortgage originator or mortgage manager.' It went on for ages with generosity and branding.

I was able to do that because I had gone through these skirmishes. I put myself out there; I'd got myself on *A Current Affair* and then I became a friend of *The Footy Show*. Every time they needed money, I would put something up, ten grand or twenty grand, and then Eddie McGuire got onto it. Eddie was looking for people to put money into the AFL *Footy Show*. I'd fly down there, to Melbourne to sit in the audience. Eddie would say things in those days you couldn't say today, 'This home loan is the best home loan in the Southern hemisphere.' I mean, talk about superlatives – in the Southern hemisphere! 'And tonight Mark Bouris, the boss of the place, the owner, is sitting in the front, and he's come down and he's going to give twenty grand away to whoever.' It was the best marketing and advertising anyone could ever do.

I put these opportunities down to a number of things, not just that we were in a position to take advantage of it. It was because I asked questions, I networked and I trusted people when I needed help. But all the TV stuff began because of two things, my friendship with David Gyngell; David was pivotal in the whole thing. He was a brilliant reader of people and the pulse of the moment. And, I took the risk and backed myself to do it. Because a lot of people wouldn't go on *The Footy Show*. I've never seen the boss of the Commonwealth Bank on *The Footy Show*. In my opinion, the leaders in big business take themselves too seriously, they're too haughty and something like *The Footy Show* is beneath them. I wasn't precious or too haughty, I was a Punchbowl boy who knew that there were many different aspects to a person and no one is better than anyone else.

To succeed in anything you have to be able to deal with any situation and being on TV was a good example of that. I had to roll with the style of the show and be whatever they needed me to be. I was able to be the character, it came naturally to me. I am a footy guy, that's my thing. And then Wizard was on the State of Origin and the footy people knew, that's Mark Bouris. The commentator, Ray Warren would say, 'That's Wizard Home Loans' and he'd give me a good rap because he knew me from *The Footy Show*. And I didn't realise it at the time, but the interconnection of all these things was crazy powerful.

•

During a period in 1999, I engaged an advertising agency and I decided to do a TV ad. What possessed me to think I'd be able to do a television ad, I've got no idea. My budget was only enough to do one month's worth of advertising on Channel 9. The agency I engaged were a reasonably small Sydney-based outfit. They hired a house in Lane Cove to use as the location. I turned up and they'd only given me a script the night before so I was trying to practise my lines and I was nervous as hell. Sitting in the backyard, live to camera, I had no idea what I was doing. I was wearing a V-neck jumper with a white t-shirt underneath, a pair of jeans and boots. In those days if anyone at a bank did an ad, they dressed in a suit, even John Symond was always seen in a suit. Banking guys wore suits. I wasn't doing that. So I was wearing a dark chocolate woollen jumper – which I still have to this day – and the white t-shirt.

The ad used imagery of David Campese playing for the Wallabies against the Barbarians, and he just did a typical David Campese thing, he somehow got the ball down on the Australian try line and he just weaved his way right through and scored a try. Then there was my voiceover and some imagery of me just sitting there in this backyard. I said that sometimes getting a home loan can be daunting, but at Wizard Home Loans we'll get you over the line. Then you see David Campese, you think it's virtually impossible for him to score, but you see him run the length of that field, jinking in and out of players.

Again, our phones went mental. In hindsight, I think it helped that I was forty years of age and dressed completely against how everyone else from the banks dressed. It looked like I was being rebellious. I wasn't, but it looked like I was. I mean, in people's minds I was rebelling against authority. I was sponsoring New South Wales rugby league, appearing on *The Footy Show* and *A Current Affair*. Now we had one month of television advertising. Business took off. In fact, our brand was far bigger than our business, much bigger than our business. So much so that it attracted the attention of John Symond and someone asked John, 'What do you think of this guy, this upstart?' John said, 'He's a disaster waiting to happen,' and it was quoted in a newspaper. That was really quite a motivational thing to happen to me. I had a point to prove now, on top of my usual determination and focus to make a business succeed.

'I want to be an upstart. If I am, I've got your attention.'

As far as I could see, I hadn't had to spend much money, relative to what John was spending at Aussie and he'd been around three or four years before me. He had a big foothold in the industry and a massive brand and he was probably making a shitload of money too. I was competition. So what he said was fair enough.

What also happened in 1999 was the tech boom. There was a lot of discussion about it around the world. I read every news item every day in those days. I read everything about what was going on in America, and the news wasn't online then. I got all the newspapers. I always subscribed to the London *Financial Times*; I used to get it delivered to my office up until six months ago. *The New York Times* and the *Wall Street Journal* were both physically delivered to me. I only bought the Friday editions of the *Financial Times* and the two American papers because Friday was for the weekend and it covered everything off for the week. Plus, there was some extra stuff in there, like lifestyle items, and I really liked that. I read those publications from front to back, and I read all our papers here. I read the *Sydney Morning Herald*. I would always try and get my hands on an *Age* if I could. I read the *Fin Review* every single day. And I watched anything I could watch on television. So, I knew what was going on in America during this tech boom. And what was going on in Australia. But I'm only ever really interested in the top five things. I'm not actually interested in knowing about everything.

'Read everything and try to find what are the common five, ten things that everyone keeps talking about.'

The top thing everyone was talking about in Australia at the time was banks closing branches. During this period, banks were closing branches all over the country. The second thing was that the Australian banks were adopting what was going on overseas. This idea that, in the future, people won't be transacting with banks at a local branch, they'll be transacting online. Rupert Murdoch started iLoan in Australia, which was an online broking portal way ahead of its time. They invested a lot of money in it, but it was too soon. You've got to bear in mind that Lachlan and James (Murdoch) were probably given the mandate, *Go out and find what's cool, what's new. What's this tech boom doing? Where should we invest? You know, like everyone's making shitloads of money out of the tech boom, how do we make money out of it?*

Do your research

This idea that everything was going to be done online for financial services was a huge narrative in America in 1999, massive. I was very interested in it and I was trying to work out what I should do. I'm a big believer in having a predictive science element in your business, trying to predict where markets are going, predict signs for our markets based on data. Today, the data is different. It's actual bits and bytes. It's much more binary, and the decisions you make are much more binary decisions: yes or no, buy or sell. In those days, though, it was about us gathering as much intelligence and understanding on what's going on, comprehending and then interpreting, and then building and understanding the most likely situations so you could find the business opportunities.

Those newspapers I would get on a Friday were particularly applicable to us and what we were doing at Wizard. I was reading everything I could, trendspotting. I'd cut the articles out, and I'd paste them in a book. I had a book of art trends and house trends, home designs and a book of business trends. I've still got them. I was following lots of journalists. You couldn't follow them online; it was a tech boom, but there was no online then. I also followed all the bank analysts and I particularly followed one analyst and his boss. The younger guy at the time, Jonathan Mott, is the number one bank analyst in the country today. He writes for UBS, a leading bank analyst and he publishes all the time.

If you're a banker and you're running a listed bank, you must appease the analyst. Because the analyst is going to rate you as buy, sell or hold. You've got to get your story through, you don't stick it up the analyst. You've got to know what the analyst wants, what the analyst's looking for. And if the analyst thinks that you're giving him what he thinks is the right way to run the bank, then you would get a buy recommendation. If you're the CEO or you're the senior manager and you're getting shares as your bonus, then your share price is going up.

It's a conflict, but that's what happens. That's human nature. The big thing at the time was the cost-to-income ratio. The analysts were at the bank saying, the rest of the world's cost-to-income ratio of running a bank is 45 per cent. But in Australia, our cost-to-income ratio was 70 per cent. It was nearly double the cost to run an Australian bank. A lot of them were government banks, so it didn't matter. The analysts in Australia were adopting the overseas analysts' views – nothing's original, it's someone else's view. Then they started writing about it here, so all the banks started madly saying, 'Shit, we're too expensive, we've got to reduce our costs.' So, banks started reducing their cost-to-income ratio. The biggest fixed cost of a bank are the bank branches. Banks would have a branch at somewhere like Padstow, because they'd always had a branch there, however most of them were customer-effective but not cost-effective.

The banks began to close branches, but they said the reason they were closing branches was because people weren't going to use branches anymore, they were going to use technology. So, it was a disconnect, but I knew that this was just spin. I thought, *Well, what I'm going to do is I'm going to open branches because people like branches, people like to know you're there and want to come in and talk to you.* So I developed a franchise model.

When you think you're done with research, do some more

I thought, *What model can I come up with to have branches, but not have the cost?* And franchising was the answer. Not many businesses in Australia did franchising at the time, especially in the hot financial services sector. Aussie didn't do it, they do it now. Rams didn't do it, but they're doing it now. None of my competitors was using franchises. I had to find a model from somewhere that worked. And there was one called 'Countrywide' in the United States.

Countrywide was a franchise-based business that became a major debacle during the GFC, but this was before that so I flew to America, went to various Countrywide branches, grabbed all their material – every brochure, photographs, everything. I brought it all back to Sydney and told my team, 'We're going to copy this to distribute our product. Because people like our brand, people will want to join us so we've got to build our brand, not just for our customers but to build our recruitment, to get people to come and join us, and build more branches. We won't charge them for the franchise. You just put the money in to run it yourself, but it's free. We won't charge a franchise fee or anything like that. And what we'll do is, we'll share with them the margin I get on a mortgage. If I make a hundred, basically 1 per cent on a mortgage, I'll give them some, and I'll take some.' My reasoning was, if I could get fifty people around the country to do what I was doing in one branch, I'd be happy to get only a small percentage. Because that's business I wouldn't get with just my branch. I knew that nothing was going to be done online anytime soon. That was still a few years

157

away. I knew the industry. It didn't matter what the banks were saying about online, it was all justification to close branches.

You can do a lot online nowadays but you can't completely transact a mortgage online. There is still a lot of heavy lifting over the other side of the phone in a room at the back. You might get onto one of those online facilities, like UBank, but then you're going to spend five hours on a telephone. But in 1999 I thought, *Well, I've got to get involved with this technology boom but, at the same time, I've got to build this franchise system.*

I decided that I was going to do an e-commerce ad. I couldn't get the name wizard.com.au, somebody had parked it, so I ended up getting the name ewizard.com.au. I thought, I'm going to launch this thing called ewizard. com.au. I knew the ad had to be different from the TV ad I'd run so I didn't use that agency again. I got Jack Singleton – John Singleton's son – and his partner, Colin Watts, they were called Jack-Watts.

I got them to come in and have a chat. They said, 'Okay we'll do the ads.' They were pretty cheap and it was just an ad for online usage, but it was on television too. There was some imagery of me – not much – and they hired a well-known surfer and a female model.

The woman had a big afro, and they talked her into shaving her hair in the ad. It was like a shower scene – you see someone shaving but you can't quite work out what's being shaved and it was very sexy. You see the woman at the beginning with all her hair and then you see her at the end with no hair. And she opens up the computer, and it says, go to ewizard.com.au. It was sort of cool and sexy.

> 'We got pulled up by the Standards Council for being too suggestive or something like that. Perfect.'

We pulled the ad, but that was all right. That was good in itself. People were talking.

In that period, we did a lot of stuff for not much money. As well as State of Origin, *The Footy Show* and *A Current Affair*, we had a couple more headlines with the *Australian Financial Review* when someone else came with a rate of 6.97 per cent and we went to 6.96 per cent. We just played the game with the newspapers. We launched an e-commerce platform. We got into trouble for launching that too. I didn't expect that to happen, but it happened.

Then, in 1999, I got a knock on the door from Australia's richest man, Kerry Packer.

BE A CONTENDER

1. Do the research. Then do more. Don't stop learning.
2. Never underestimate the value of networking and asking questions.
3. If people do the wrong thing by you, tell them! And don't stifle your anger if it is deserved. Be assertive and don't back down. Hold people to account – including yourself.
4. Sometimes you have to spend your own money to make something happen.
5. Keep an eye on trends and predictions of new technologies. Be ready to act fast.

ROUND SEVEN

The Dark Arts of Business War

People who work with me probably call me a lot of things but a shrinking violet isn't one of them. I know what I want done, and I know how I want it done, and I have absolutely no problem telling people. That is one of my key pieces of advice: ditch the wishy-washy stuff and embrace your brutal side to get shit done and get it done right.

Fighting dirty

A couple of years ago I had to defend a takeover of my company, Yellow Brick Road. The way it generally works is that the aggressor – the person making the takeover bid – needs to get shareholders to accept a bid and convince them that the person defending the bid – in this case, me – is no good. They do this through all sorts of means available – through media, through networks through whispered conversations, however they can. I can tell you, it isn't pleasant to be on the receiving end of an aggressive bid, and this one was aggressive and offered a very low price. I sat there facing bad media and a lot of times because of the way the media stories are placed, I was always on the back foot. Once a story's out, you can't defend it. The person who wrote the story isn't going to write another story. The moment has passed. You might go to another publication and get another story written, you might be successful in that, but usually once a story's written no one else wants to write anything new about it.

So a non-friendly takeover was launched – they attacked me when I wasn't ready. They were trying to take over my whole business at a ridiculously low price.

They weren't successful. By the way, that is our market so I'm not complaining.

I have experienced an attack from that point of view before. It's effective because you're not prepared for it but, equally, it can motivate you. So it motivated me to be prepared. I'm always prepared for that kind of attack now. Always. For an unfriendly takeover, always. There are different ways you prepare for it, but I'm always onto it. So, I've experienced that.

If the opponent fights dirty in business, it usually ends up in the media environment and that can affect your reputation.

'There's an old Jewish saying, *"tov shem mi'shemen tov"* which means "oil is good but reputation is best".'

When you've got a brand out there built upon your own personal reputation, a business brand which has been built over a twenty-five-year period, an attack on your reputation is hurtful. The only response you've got is to fight back with the same dirty methods, which means garnering every favour and coming up with every possible way of attacking the person who's attacking you.

If someone fights dirty with me in the boxing ring I'll fight dirty back. If someone starts to hold my neck or the back of my head, there's a whole lot of things I can do in boxing that are dirty. If they hit you with their shoulder when you get in close and get up underneath you, I will do that back with interest. If they do one thing dirty to me I will double down on it in the boxing ring. And I will do that in business to you.

Jeff Fenech once had a bloke who wanted to do some sparring, I don't know exactly what the backstory was and I certainly didn't know the guy. Jeff turned up to the gym with the bloke, and said, 'Mark, you're sparring with this bloke today.' I said, 'No drama.' We started sparring and this guy got a bit serious, we were only sparring but he threw a few, clubbed me a bit and I didn't like it. When you're sparring you're not supposed to try and knock each other out. These are the unwritten rules and I'm happy to abide by them. Well, he started to get on my nerves and actually whacked me a few times, which I considered inappropriate when sparring. I looked across at Jeff and I could see he knew that I was getting a bit pissed off. But, out of respect to Jeff, because he'd brought the guy along, I let things ride. This guy carried on and after a while I'd had enough and I just thought, *Fuck it*. I remember hitting him with my left hand, he went reeling back pretty hard. But I wasn't going to stop and I jumped all over him. Jeff tells the story that they had to pull me off, because as this bloke was going down I was still hitting him to make sure he kept going down.

My view is that if someone attacks you, you're entitled to attack back and you should attack twice as hard. But you should never attack first. There's no point holding back. It's the same in business. If somebody attacks me in business – I don't mean says something on Instagram or Twitter, I'm talking about actually tries to dethrone me or attacks the integrity of my business or tries to unpick it or steal a staff member – I will turn on them 100 per cent.

'You pull the cat's tail you get the whole fucking cat.'

That's what I believe and that's how I operate. You pull my tail, I'm not just going to tuck my tail away, I'm going to fucking jump all over you. You've got to be like that in business. You have to be. It is all or nothing. I've worked too hard to surrender, ever!

The franchise system ended up being pretty effective for me at Wizard and soon other businesses, like Aussie Home Loans, tried to recruit people from my team. John Symond and I are competitors so we watch what each other's company does. He saw what Wizard was doing and I am sure he put pressure on his people to grow his business. I would have. They had a good footprint but I had a much bigger footprint than them in terms of branches. So, their recruitment people would go to a Wizard branch, knock on the door and ask, 'How are you going? Would you like to join us at Aussie?' My loyal people would ring me and tell me they'd been approached by Aussie. Within half a day my lawyers had a letter in the hands of John Symond saying cease and desist, if you don't we'll be taking you to court for encouraging somebody to breach their contract.

I can't remember the exact terms but I was prepared to go on with it, there was no bluff. I was deadly serious. Usually we'd get a call from someone saying, 'Oh, no, we're not trying to do that, it's my people who did it, I'll tell them to stop that.' But I would have carried that through right to the end, no problem whatsoever. I was all over it, and that's the only way I operate. Again, it's business so I am not complaining.

Because I'm pretty aware of this idea myself, I've never pulled a cat's tail unless I was ready for the consequences. I know what I would do so I don't try to do that to anybody else.

I told the cat's tail story to my Wizard people. So they would be that way too. They pull that tail, we all jump over it, every one of us. All together. This is army stuff, this is real battle stuff.

For me the business world is like kingdoms and battles with strategies and processes. If there's an opponent there and they're trying to do the wrong thing, how do I undermine them in every way possible? It's not just my front line people who shoot the arrows and a few people with spears who attack, I'm trying to think about how we come in behind them while they're distracted with what's in front of them too. You've got to defend your kingdom. And that's why people come and join me, because they know I'll defend them. It's not just about them advancing and doing well, it's about who's going to defend them when something goes wrong. Who will have their back? That's what I have to do and it's important to me that I always look after the people who work with me.

Don't nobble anyone else's business

If someone's got a good business, good luck to them. I don't try and take what anyone else has got. I never have. To me that's tantamount to theft.

> 'Build your own game, there's enough
> out there for everybody.'

Just go about your business, that's the way I operate. Kerry Packer once said to me, 'Son, I don't really like what your competitors are doing with the banks.' Aussie was attacking the banks, left, right and centre. 'I don't want you to do that at Wizard.' I had no intention of doing that anyway but having him explain why it was a bad idea just reinforced that intention.

He said, 'I'll ask you one question. Where does an eight-hundred-pound gorilla shit?' That was the question. I thought, *In the woods? I don't know.* He said, 'Wherever it fucking wants.' He said, 'They – the banks – are eight-hundred-pound gorillas and they'll shit on you if you start giving them a hard time. Why attract attention? Just get your market share. If you can get six to seven per cent of the total market, you've killed it. You're never going to get twenty-five or thirty per cent.'

It was great advice. My enemy are my competitors but I never attacked Aussie Home Loans. I never attacked Rams. I never attack the banks, ever. I never said bad things about the banks to build the Wizard brand, never, ever. Why should I? I'm just putting a target on my back and they're big, they can crush you if they want to. On your way up, there's no point putting a target on yourself because the best time for them to get you is on your way up, that's the beginning.

In rugby union, New Zealand, the All Blacks, are famous for their pre-game haka. Every opponent over the years has tried every which way to respond, many confrontationally. The Kiwis want a reaction to the haka, they want their opponents to be off their game. Just stand there respectfully and let your football do the talking later. Don't react to it because they know that they've got in your head if you do. You can't let anyone know that they've got in your head.

That's why trash-talking is silly. I don't mind it if it's for fun and entertainment, UFC Conor McGregor–style, that's okay, but I don't want too much of it. I don't believe in doing it myself.

Many years ago, I was in a car park. I'd bought myself a new car, I was about thirty maybe. I was very fit and I'd had my fair share of fights in the ring. I drove into this car park, reversed my car in. This guy came flying down the ramp and just clipped the front of my brand-new convertible. I was enraged. I got out of my car and I was yelling and screaming at him to stop, get out of the fucking car, and all this sort of stuff. The guy did stop, he got out of his car and it felt like it took him a minute because he just kept unfolding, bigger and bigger and bigger. He was like a giant. I thought, *Shit, I've gone this far I have to go him.* And I walked up to him and said something, had a crack at him and he just said, 'What are you going to do about it?' Just like that. I took a swing at him and I hit him right on the chin. His head went back but he didn't move. I thought, *Fuck, I'm in trouble here.* I woke up in hospital, I had concussion and I was vomiting and suffered a headache for two days. I was hospitalised for nearly three days. I learned my lesson. The same applies in business.

'Pick a fight but pick a fight where you've got a chance.'

If you're not ready to fight, don't fight. There's no point going into it because you're going to lose. You've got to learn to pick your fights. It's just like Kerry said, 'Don't go picking on big institutions, you're not going to beat 'em.'

Businesses can't beat government restrictions at the moment. I'm not saying, give up though – there's a big difference. If you're in it, you're in it. If that car park thing had happened the other way around, if he'd got out first and was going to confront me, I wouldn't have run. I'll fight whoever or whatever but I don't go starting it anymore. There's no point starting a fight you can't win.

I'm not saying give up, but direct your energy into things you *can* win. And your energy is precious, it is what can drive you to success.

I hear businesspeople talking about fatigue. Fatigue's a state of mind. I can feel fatigue, but I know to change my mindset. So if you feel fatigue do something that will change your mindset. What is it for you? Is it a simple day at the beach or is it going on a picnic with somebody and seeing nature? Learn some techniques to actually help revive you to get over fatigue. Unless you're absolutely physically fatigued because you're working a seventeen-hour day. But if it's emotional, mental – then you need to refresh yourself.

If you can't get a good night's sleep, work out how to fix that. Would taking a melatonin tablet help? I'm a big believer in nootropics, supplements that aid cognitive function. If you're chemically low, you can't change your state of mind so find out what helps you revitalise yourself or re-energise yourself, or helps you change your state of mind. Eat well, exercise, rest, rejuvenate and keep yourself in shape to win any battle, physically and mentally. And know that we all face challenges sometimes.

We all doubt ourselves at some point

I do. To be honest, I doubt myself at least once or twice a month. It happens, but it doesn't happen for very long. I have techniques. I'll think, *I haven't had any sunlight, I need to get some sunlight. I haven't been in nature.* To me nature's really important, I've got to get into a garden or I've got to walk through a garden or just go for a walk in nature. Maybe I haven't done enough exercise, I haven't been able to get those endorphins into my system, those chemicals. I'm chasing chemicals all the time. Natural chemicals. Energy is about chemicals and I've got to get the chemistry right. I know when my hormones are down. If that doesn't work, then what other things can I do? Have I not interacted with enough people, have I not seen enough people? Have I had enough laughter? Have

I not had enough wins, have I not seen my football team win? What are all the things I need to get my head right? And then I just keep pushing, trying different things. Going in different directions. It might take me a day or two, but I get there eventually. It could be that I've just not had enough sleep.

I don't look at myself as being emotional, I'm just a bag of chemistry and my energy comes from those chemical reactions. It's pretty simple. What are the chemical reactions that I'm missing? I know I can feel good, so what are the things I was doing when I felt good, what do I have to bring back in balance?

It sounds very simple and perhaps cold-hearted. I don't know if this works for everybody, but as far as I am concerned we are all a whole set of chemical reactions. So get yourself balanced and get your head right. If you can't do it yourself, then see your doctor and get professional advice and help to strengthen your body and your mind. You can't rise up if you aren't in shape.

Treachery in business

I've read Sun Tzu's *The Art of War* so many times. I hand that book around with stuff underlined. Same with Machiavelli's *The Prince*, I used to underline specific lines and hand it on to my main people, and I'd get them to underline what they responded to and then hand it on to the next person, so you'd read what someone else thought was important. What was in red was so and so, what was in blue was mine, what was in black was the next person. Everybody gets to see what someone else sees as important. I love that sort of psychology. *Game of Thrones* was just brilliant to me because I was interested in the treachery and the backstabbing and the jealousies. Watch these shows and movies, put these books on your list and keep them close to hand, don't just hide them away on a bookshelf and pretend you read them.

Maybe it's because my ancestry is Greek and somewhere along the line I'm descended from the House of Atreus, but I get intrigued by power and treachery. How people can turn on each other, families, brothers and sisters or husbands, wives or friends. Father against son. How treachery can eclipse loyalty and family values. It's as old as time itself. Why does it happen? Power, ambition, greed. Those deadly sins eclipse real values to me. Real standards. Then people get confused. I believe that's what happens in politics today – the power's there for the wrong reasons.

There were people like Rasputin, they were evil because they knew exactly what they were doing and why they were doing it. Those types of people exist today. I don't like the way people like that think, but I am intrigued by them. Actors always want to play those parts, so I'm not the only one who's curious. They're always the more interesting people to play. Everyone wants to play Iago in *Othello*. Much more fun. The thing is, those characters, those people, think they're right.

You can even look at the Greek gods. In all the stories about the Greek gods, there were always bad Greek gods who were doing things like killing their children. The treachery that existed right back then still exists today. We all pretend to be more refined but, really, have we changed?

One thing that particularly intrigues me is treachery in business.

I experienced it first-hand when the GFC occurred and General Electric – who had bought Wizard – decided to get out of financial services. I see that as a treacherous period in my life.

To me, it was the system that created this treachery and people fitted into it. It was a period where people were forced to create a perception that they were fixing the problem created by the GFC and the way they did it was to undermine others. Not many people have ever experienced the might of General Electric, one of the world's most profitable companies. They were the world's largest company until Exxon overtook them. I experienced it. They weren't evil, but they had to act that way. That's what business does.

To some extent I was probably guilty of being treacherous during my ambitious mid-twenties. The coup I orchestrated at the accounting firm was an act of treachery. It is one of the biggest mistakes I've ever made. Not only did I make a bad commercial mistake, but I did the wrong thing. I still regret it today.

Sometimes these dynasties in life and business are the natural course of things. The new young usurper overthrowing the power that has been sitting there getting fat for too long. It poses a good question.

'Do you have to be a cunt to be successful?'

I think Rupert Murdoch once said you don't have to be a cunt to be successful. I don't know if that's true from his point of view but let's posit this pithy question another, perhaps more elegant, way: To be the best at what you want to be in business, do you have to give everything of what you've got and be prepared to do whatever it takes?

Probably. I think to be honest you probably do.

Do you have to be prepared to stab people in the back and cut their throats and stamp on their feet? (If you look at all these Netflix series they're all about that.) To answer that, the question then becomes: Do you have to be ruthless in your commitment? Ruthless in every aspect, so you don't care about other people's feelings, or can you do it in another way? Can you care about people's feelings and still be successful?

I am ruthless. I'm always looking for weaknesses. While I know I am generous and lots of other good things, I am also fucking ruthless. I take the view that I need to know everything about my potential enemies. Everything. I'll pay to find out. I've had people investigated to get the information I need. If there's somebody in my own business I don't trust then I'll get an audit done on their computer. I'll know everything that's been said and done, because it's my computer anyway. Read the fine print of your employment contract. An employer can access your emails! I'll do whatever it takes forensically, find out everything I need to know. So, I am ruthless in that respect. I find out everything I need to know.

You have to be ruthless in terms of your discipline, ruthless in terms of your purpose.

Have I found a line that I won't cross? In my older years, yes. This implies that in my younger years I wasn't so mindful of crossing these lines.

Would I have been able to get where I am today had I not been like that? That's a good question. I don't know the answer. If I knew then what I know now I could probably do it without crossing those lines but that's not how life works, is it?

> 'I definitely would be in some people's black books and it doesn't bother me in the least.'

I'm not a guilty-conscience type of person. I don't have that sort of Catholic guilt, even though I am Catholic, it just doesn't exist in me. I have regrets. I have done things in a certain way, mainly when I was impetuous, or young, that I wish I hadn't. I wish I had gone about some things in business in different ways, not because I've hurt somebody necessarily. I don't really care what they feel but I don't want to do things by hurting or taking advantage of somebody, I'd rather do them in a more intelligent way.

I don't mean covert or hidden actions though. I'll stand up and own things. Although I will do things in a secretive manner so that I don't alert my enemy. Yet, at the end, I'll still say, that was me, my signature was on your death warrant. If I'm marching out to hunt down my quarry with an army I'll be at the front of the army.

I'm not going to be standing in the shadows, that's not my style. Even if I knew I was going down and there was no way out of it, I'd fight to the death. You have to care about what you do, to do that.

Literature is an unsung hero

I'm watching a TV series at the moment called *The Last Kingdom*, it's about Alfred the Great and how he withstood the Danish incursions. Within Alfred's own family his wife, son and daughter are all treacherous at some point and they're fighting over kingdoms and queendoms. It's about places like Wessex and Mercia, it's quite fascinating in a historical sense.

I am not saying you have to be treacherous to be successful in business, but people who are really successful in business think these things through – not in terms of an empire, that word has bad connotations – but in terms of how do I build something that's lasting and big and has momentum? Generally speaking it means you've got to build a bit of a kingdom. And you've got to be ruthless in your focus in that regard.

The odds are, the more successful you are someone's going to try and take it away from you. Just like in all those stories from the past, there may not be dragons but too often someone is always trying to take something away from someone else. Those stories are still accurate reflections of society today. Nothing's changed.

You've got to understand the truth behind mythical stories and understand that they reflect a very real side of human nature. If you want to run your business successfully just think about how people really are. If you haven't thought about that then you can't run your business well.

'If you want to know how I run a business, how I recruit people and how I build retention and loyalty – well go and read a few old mythological stories, go and study *Game of Thrones* because they're a better way of learning how to run your business than half of the how-to-run-your-business books out there.'

You have to get people on side. You have to respect how they feel and what their motivations are and understand how that can impact on the day-to-day running of a business. Often people will stab each other in the back on the way through, they'll create problems for you, they'll try to wish you down. There will be power struggles, all small scale but it's the same deal. It's totally the same deal. I find it fascinating.

Enjoy knowing these things and observing everything about your business in those terms. Building a successful business is not just about the maths, the logistics, the equipment you have, the physical infrastructure you put in place, it is also about the psychology of the people you work with, the people you employ, the people you deal with. You need to know these people well and understand the impact they have or could have, both positively and negatively and make sure that you are getting the most positive behaviours coming your way. Know what people are about, especially when you're talking to younger people. One of the things I love about working with the younger people in my businesses generally is they're smart, ambitious, skilled, tough, but they're not life experienced. It's quite interesting to observe as they learn on the job. I love being in business with them, watching them.

Adapt or die

Being in business means pivoting all the time.

I stood for this slogan 'Every Australian deserves good quality advice' and I ran that for seven years. It turns out the government legislation has changed and the regulatory environment makes it too expensive for me to hand that advice out anymore. I can't do it and make money. I had to pivot off that and just do mortgages. But it was a dream of mine to give advice, to help out every Australian, help them with their superannuation and give them the advice they need to make better financial choices up until the day they retired. And that they retired in a positive financial position after working their whole life for this moment.

But markets change – we know that so pointedly today – so I had to change the way I went about my business. That's a pivot. It took me a year to adapt my business to a new environment. I had to move staff on. I had to pull down all my defences and I had to reshape the whole business. Completely. I had to sell off assets and things that I would no longer use, make staff redundant, cut my costs. That's an example of me pivoting. It was tough but for a business to survive it has to constantly adapt and you have to be ruthless about the decisions you make and put the survival of the business above everything.

You can never prepare enough

Everything I do is always about preparation. I drive my senior management mad because I'm always asking, 'Hang on, have we looked at this?' and I'm sure they're not thinking about it as an issue. I remember one stage during the Wizard business, someone wanted to put money into our business, but we didn't need it, we had plenty of money at the time. Kerry (Packer) said to me, 'You know what? We should take that money because I can tell you now, Mark, when you need the money you won't be able to get it and when you don't need it, it's available.' There's only one way around that, you take it when you don't need it because sooner or later you will. I said it earlier, take the money.

For me, that's part of always being 'prepared', always being 'on the ready', because when the time comes you won't be able to do those things quickly enough if you are under pressure.

Regrets, I've had a few

The biggest mistake or the biggest issue I wrestle with is thinking about all the deals I was going to do but didn't. Does this mean that I'm my own worst enemy? No, I've just had to learn how to stop thinking about them, to forget about them.

From time to time, I think, *I had that idea, now someone else has done it, I should have done it myself.* Should-have, could-have, who gives a fuck! But I do go through those processes. I'm always rinsing my brain out. I do it every week. I have regrets, every week, but they don't last long. I don't dwell on them but I acknowledge them. It helps keep me on my toes. But then I come back to this: think about what you are doing, what you're doing well, or what you have done and just continue. That is important, keep going, don't get bogged down in regret or fear. Be bold and march on.

FACING CHALLENGES AND ENEMIES

1. Be honourable in business, but if someone comes at you be ready to fight. They hit you, you hit harder.
2. Don't start a fight you can't win – it'll only waste the energy you could have spent on driving towards success.
3. Never let on that someone has got to you.
4. Don't think you can sit back and bask in your success forever. Sure, celebrate the wins, but keep your eye on the business or project at all times – be ready to adapt to the unexpected.
5. Take care of the people you work with.

Heavyweight

I didn't go hunting Kerry Packer. I never thought about him for a second. I never had investment from him as a possibility in my mind even though I was running out of money. John Symond at Aussie Home Loans had Macquarie Bank behind him. The guy behind Rams – John Kinghorn – was rich and much older than me. I didn't have anybody and my partners had no money to help back us up. So, I knew I needed a partner, a backer, but I didn't know where I was going to get one. I certainly didn't think of Kerry Packer, ever.

It was James Packer who was on the hunt, like Lachlan Murdoch was too. Young men looking to prove themselves. I understood that. And the original hunt came because they had a company called ecorp of which PBL (Publishing and Broadcasting Limited) was the biggest shareholder. The company was listed to the public and the head of that company was Daniel Petre, who was an ex-managing director from Microsoft, and a guy called Jeremy Phillips, who was also from Microsoft. In those days, they were full-on tech heads, global leaders in technology, relative to what we were doing in Australia.

At the time, they needed assets in ecorp, so they bought Charles Schwab in Australia, they owned eBay here, and they thought financial services were going to take off because there was a lot of liquidity in the world, a lot of money had to find a place to be lent to and a lot of it was finding its way into Australian mortgages. That would have been the advice they were getting, so they were looking at companies like my company.

I'm a big supporter of the Sydney Roosters NRL club and I met Nick Politis, who was the club's chairman, through a whole series of circumstances. I don't even remember exactly how, it might've been talking about Wizard as a potential sponsor. We became friends and Nick and David Gyngell were very close too. Nick is eighty now, but in his younger days he was a very vibrant guy, full-on. He still is, actually. He invited me to the Roosters' games. So there I was in the Chairman's Club –

you had to pay for it, it was five or six grand a year at the time – and James Packer was on the board of the Roosters, as was David Gyngell, and he used to come to the games.

I was already friends with David and I soon became friends with James. He invited me around to his house a few times with a whole lot of others. You know, we were young so we'd go around to his place, have a few beers, dinner, hang out. I remember he said to me one day, after we'd had a few beers, 'Mate, my family is looking at buying into Aussie Home Loans or Rams. We're in solid deep talks with them, you're in this business, what would you be asking them if you were buying? They're telling me all this shit I need to know, but what is it that I don't know and that I should be asking them about?' And I started talking about things like margins and liquidity, those sorts of things, just the fundamentals of running a securitised business. Rams was securitising, Aussie was not. Aussie was leaving all the securitisation to Macquarie Bank, but Aussie was reselling that money as an Aussie Home Loans product.

I thought about it the next day. What crossed my mind at the time, to be honest with you, was just to bag Aussie and Rams, to put them down, but I couldn't put the boot into my opposition. That wouldn't be right and there is a difference between ruthless and right. Aussie Home Loans and Rams were much bigger brands than me, they were big businesses, and the Packers were big guys. The thought did cross my mind, *Well, maybe he'd be interested in investing in me.* But my thought process was that he wouldn't be interested in investing in me because he was going for the big names. Packer's a big-name investor, lots of firepower. Why would he go for a smaller brand? Those days, in terms of volume, I was easily third best. So I didn't say anything to him, I didn't express the thought. But I knew there were more conversations to be had. My company fitted the bill and I was cheaper than Aussie Home Loans. Aussie, as a business, would have been much more complex than mine because it's much bigger. And I was open to it.

> 'It's a vital marketing tool, the ability to assess
> whether this is a position where you promote
> yourself or hold back ... hold or play, it's poker.'

I had a few more beers and a few more discussions with James over the next couple of weeks, then one day he asked me, 'Why am I buying into these two guys, why don't I just buy your business?'

I said, 'I'm not for sale.'

They were obviously looking for a partner. Everyone was looking for a partner. We all needed money.

'But I might sell half,' I added.

From there, the process started. Once you're in the process, you're part of a machine.

It was time for another coup, but it was properly thought out and logical this time. It wasn't about ego, it was about good business. I didn't get everyone together in a restaurant and tell them what was going to happen. It wasn't perfect, but I held a board meeting – there were five of us, four of the original brokers and me. I had a 40 per cent share in the company, and they had 60 per cent between them, but most of the 60 per cent was held by one guy.

The business was already called Wizard Home Loans. They'd already set up a budget, detailed forecasting and a business plan. We'd done a bit of advertising, for which I was the sole investor. I'd paid for all the advertising. I'd lent our company $250,000 to make that happen. So I explained, 'You guys don't put any money in, but if I'm going to do this, if it takes off and does really well, you know, we've got to expand the business and we've got to borrow some money. We've got to be ready to expand and build this business up to be a really *big* business. And there's already a lot of money for me to get back.' I was worried I wouldn't get the return I needed, and certainly not my $250,000, because I wasn't running the business. I was a 40 per cent shareholder but I wasn't there every day. I needed to get involved so I said to them, 'I need to know that the business has the mindset that it's going to take advantage of whatever comes from that big investment. That's a significant amount of money.'

The response was muted and that worried me. The other shareholders wanted to wait and just see how it went. I didn't want to wait, I wanted to grow the business at a faster rate so I called for a vote.

There were two young guys and two older guys in the company with me. The two older guys were making a good living, they were paying their mortgages off, and had nice lifestyles so I wasn't sure they would be up for change. To go through with this plan of mine, we had to have a special resolution and more than 75 per cent of shareholders had to vote in favour of it. We had a vote, the two youngsters voted in my favour, the big shareholder voted in my favour, but the other guy voted against. He had enough votes, more than 25 per cent, to stop a special resolution.

I was pretty filthy. This was an opportunity, big time and it was being stymied.

The majority of the people who were in the business every day wanted to go in the direction I wanted to take the business. We were united on that. So, in my mind, there was only one way around this: get rid of him.

The bloke went home that night, it was a Friday, and I packed up all his shit. Put it in a box, locked the door, changed the locks on the front door. Booted him out.

Was I allowed to do that? Probably not. He went to our lawyers, got a court order and an injunction against me. We weren't allowed to carry on business until it was resolved. Obviously he had grounds, he wouldn't have got the injunction otherwise. He had enough legally to stop me, he had more than 25 per cent. But I knew that everybody else wanted to do what I wanted to do and he was going against the majority.

I'm not vicious. To me, the numbers were similar to the accounting business coup; to me, it's all bullshit. Where does it say who owns a client? Just because you own more shares in a company, the legal people say that you have that position, the judge will say you've got that position, but it's legal fiction in my opinion. In a practical sense, in a business sense, if the rest of us decide we don't want to go in your direction but you veto a majority decision then it's fiction. If it came down to it, what would happen if we all walked out and just started up again the next day with a new business?

It took a couple of weeks to get sorted. The court ordered us to mediation. He had his lawyers and accountants and I appointed my lawyer, a guy called Mark O'Brien. He was the guy who won the Super League war case for the ARL. The deal ended up with me buying the other guy out. It was done. I took some of the shares that I bought from him and gave them to the two young guys as they'd shown they were hungry and onboard with my vision for the company. The third guy was a little bit diluted, but he was happy with the deal anyway. Knowing that I had the chance to make the business bigger meant I had to make these moves. If I'd hesitated, we would have lost momentum. You have to know when to make a strategic move and then back yourself to make it happen. I did that with no regrets. And in the end, we all won.

Can you teach someone how to become an entrepreneur?

People often ask me to guide them, to tell them what to do. I don't like to do that in a prescriptive way. What I want to do is fire up people to think like an innovator. I'm not even sure I like the word entrepreneur. There are courses now at universities on how to be an entrepreneur, but there are some things in business, like these skirmishes I just mentioned above, that can't be taught. Sure, there's lots of stuff that can be taught and that's important to learn, like structure and framework. Leonardo da Vinci sketched anatomy for decades and decades but no one could teach him how to paint the *Mona Lisa* or *The Last Supper*. Some things are just not on the curriculum, some moves – most of which are gutsy – are inspirational. They are not teachable.

This particular skirmish didn't have the intellectual arrogance afterburn of the previous coup at the accounting firm. I'd learned my lesson. On that one, I did what I wanted to do, but what I didn't see, what I couldn't see or, more pointedly, wasn't willing to see in my eagerness to keep going, was something massive that I may have missed out on. That didn't happen this time. I wasn't brash or speedy. I moved quickly, but I had the best lawyer this time. He was unbelievable.

James Packer had said, 'I'm not going to deal with rats and mice, mate, buy them all out.' So, I bought everybody out. I bought them all out and then I gave them shares back. I gave them synthetic equity behind the wall. So, James doesn't see what's behind the wall, he just sees me. That's where all my experience with structured business from the law firm work became very handy. I could do a deal like that. James was dealing with me alone. He never met the others, never talked to them.

So ecorp bought 25 per cent of my business, and PBL bought the other 25 per cent. PBL controlled ecorp as well. James and I were now 50/50 in the business. The others sat behind the wall, and I held their shares for them. That would never have worked with the other guy who was there. So that's what happened.

•

This was a new era. When ecorp came on as shareholders, they assisted in appointing a CEO, a CFO and I was made chairman. We had board meetings every month. There was lots of structure – we had to report back to them as shareholders, every month they had their people on my board.

It was a change, but it was good. It felt great because I got $25 million to spend on marketing and branding and I had access to all the PBL assets at the most favoured nation rates. That's a big deal. *The Footy Show* got hyped up. I was on *Burke's Backyard*, I was on *Backyard Blitz, Renovation Rescue*; every show that had anything to do with property, I was on it. I'd have to give some money away, but it'd come out of the $25 million that I'd raised. It was good financial engineering from their point of view; they invested $25 million of capital that goes on their balance sheet as an asset, $25 million into my business. I then spend half of the $25 million with them in advertising. So, they turned capital into revenue, plus they still owned the asset. If you think about it, the asset's going up in value, so it will be going better if we're doing a good job in promoting the brand and generating business.

James and all the lawyers in the room took me to a certain point, the deal was all done, everything was agreed, ready to sign and then I learned that the last part of the deal was to be done with Kerry Packer. I had to go and see him at the last second, on the last day. 'Just spend a bit of time with him,' they said.

Make yourself accountable

I had met Kerry Packer before, but I couldn't say I knew him well. I mean, he wouldn't have known who I was. I might've met him at a function or something like that.

This was 1999. And we're talking specifically about July or August 1999. The way things work in those organisations is you do the deal with everybody. I did the deal with James after many, many months of due diligence and questions from his lawyers, and bankers, and accountants, and everyone else. And then you think you're done and you breathe that sigh of relief and the adrenaline drops off, and then you get told, 'You've got to go meet Kerry Packer.' I had no idea that was going to happen, because I'd never been through that process before. I probably should've kept a little bit of energy in my tank, but I didn't and I was actually, to be honest with you, quite relieved that the deal was done so it was a bit of a letdown to learn it wasn't.

I got told on the Friday, 'The deal is done. Everything is finished, complete, we're going to do the deal with you next week,' and then I had to go see Kerry on the Monday.

The story is worth some theatre in the telling, at least the theatre of my best recollection, and we know how recollections can work. To some extent we probably tend to embellish and dramatise the memory a bit. But this is my memory of how it went.

I had to go to 54 Park Street, which was the legendary Consolidated Press Holdings headquarters, known as the Packer 'Tower of Power', overlooking Sydney's Hyde Park. Park Street was the location of the original offices of Sir Frank Packer's *Daily Telegraph*. I was told to go to level three. On the morning in question I was very nervous and I made sure that I had myself properly attired.

> 'It's the pitch of your life. You're going to do the biggest, most important pitch of your life.'

To me, Kerry Packer was more like a myth or a legend than a real person. All I knew was what I had read about him in the press and what I'd seen on television. There was no Google in those days, there was none of that type of research, but nonetheless I definitely knew all about the man. He was larger than life in my mind. And, of course, everything was riding on this meeting with him.

I turned up, went up to level three and told the receptionist I was there to meet Kerry Packer. I had to wait. It seemed like I waited for hours. It was at least an hour and a half. He was late. But what am I going to do? I'm not going to storm out and say, 'How dare he?' I was a forty-year-old guy about to receive a very large cheque into my company and bring on a new partner. I had so much invested in this deal, I was so far into it that I was never going to leave. I was hardly likely to move a muscle.

I waited and waited and then Kerry walked in. He saw me. He just looked at me and he pointed to where he wanted me to go down to his office. He said there was a corridor I had to walk down, a long corridor past his secretary. I walked into his office and it was like you would expect, I wasn't one bit disappointed. It was all timber and elegant carpet, big chairs and lots of books and photographs of famous people, and artwork. It looked like the office of a media magnate. Just like out of a movie. *Citizen Kane* stuff. He wasn't there at that point, he'd ushered me in that direction and so I had done as I was told. And then he arrived. And it was theatrical in my memory, but my gut feeling is he worked the theatre. I mean, let's face it, he was in the media. He owned media. He knew theatre and I don't think he was putting on theatre for me personally; I think that everything he did was theatre. Either that or he was just naturally theatrical, one of the two.

Eventually, Kerry sat down behind this massive desk. I was standing on the other side of the desk waiting to be offered a seat, which eventually happened. I sat down, and the chair I was on was small, very small, relative to his chair, to his desk, to the size of the room. It wouldn't be a lie to say I felt like Little Miss Muffet sitting on her tuffet. That's how it felt to me. Okay, that's an exaggeration, but I did have the feeling that I was rather insignificant. That feeling probably had something to do with my own complexities, because I was in there with a big dog; to me he was the big dog.

He didn't say much, he just sort of stared at me. Kerry Packer had a penetrating glare that looked right through you. It was like he was reading your thoughts, reading your insecurities. That's what it felt like. He called for his secretary and she walked in, lit his cigarette, and walked out again. I thought that was extraordinary, but he was old school. That's just the relationship he had with this particular secretary at the time. Some people would gasp and say, 'That's not correct,' but it was what it was and I just accepted it. It was more theatre. I took a gulp of air. I felt that air going to my stomach. All of this was a demonstration of power. I don't mean he was doing it on purpose, but it was demonstrably powerful from his point of view relative to me.

I could feel the pressure on my neck, shoulders and head. He smoked his cigarette and continued to just stare at me. Didn't say a word, didn't smile, he gave me nothing. I had nothing to work with. Zero. Not even a movement. He just smoked his cigarette like he was enjoying it, as though I was not even in the room. Yet he was still looking at me. He was like a dog sleeping, like a big guard dog sleeping. You know the dog's sleeping, but you also know that he's completely aware that you are there. And if you make one wrong move, within a split second that dog could bite you. That's how I felt. It was intimidating.

Eventually he put the cigarette out in an enormous, spotless ashtray and he asked, 'What did you think of the process?'

I replied, 'Well, I had everybody look at it and you managed to grind the price down to a much lower number, which I guess is what due diligence is all about. That's the whole reason it's designed a certain way. Your people did a good job.'

He said, 'We got the value of the business that we're buying into down by fifty per cent.' He was talking about my business.

'I know,' I said.

'You happy with that?'

'I'm happy with that.'

He asked, 'You happy with the terms and conditions?' The contract was there, it was ridiculously complex.

'Yeah, I'm happy with it.' What could I do? I didn't want to change it. I didn't say that, but that's what I was thinking.

And then he said, 'Well, that's all well and good, but now I'm about to do my due diligence.'

Kerry Packer had this ability to cut your feet from underneath you, so you'd land on your arse. He set me up by asking was I happy with this, that and the other. I said I was, and then he said, 'Well, now you're going to go through it again, but this time I'm going to be doing the asking.' This was a demonstration of power. He was not trying to be a bully, this was not bully stuff – this was true power, intellectual power, experiential power of somebody who knew what it was he needed to know.

All the other stuff was just peripheral. He knew there was something he needed to know that he hadn't been told yet and he just got straight to the point. He was very economical in terms of the words he used and where he went to with things. He said, 'I've got three questions for you.'

Three questions that changed my business

The first question he asked was:

'What business are you in?'

My business was called Wizard Home Loans. For me, it was pretty obvious what business I was in. I was in the business of home loans, because it was in my business name, Wizard Home Loans. There'd been three months of due diligence on the home loan market, our interest rates, our profit margins and our volume. It was all about home loans, it was pretty obvious. And we were in the media so I assumed he would know who we were. But then I was somewhat discombobulated because I thought, *Maybe he doesn't know who we are?* When you go to a meeting with somebody who is about to invest in your business and you think they don't know who you are, that's a bit disconcerting. That's a big *oh, shit* worry, because you're hoping they're sold on you already, they want to close off the deal. I looked at him and, before I could answer that question, within three or four seconds of me about to say it, he said, 'Don't say fucking home loans.'

Of course, that's the answer I was going to give him. So now I didn't know what to answer. I didn't know the answer to the very first question of due diligence that Kerry Packer asked me on the day that I was about to collect the cheque and bank it into our business. Another *oh, shit* thought went through my mind. This time it was accompanied by, *I've failed.* Thoughts were flying through my mind pretty quickly, but I'd stuffed the first question, fallen at the first fence. I didn't know the answer. I didn't know what business I was in.

I didn't have a clue, and he said, 'Listen, I like you. I like businesses like yours, you're disrupting the market, you're taking on the big players.' He continued, 'I'm going to tell you what sort of business you're in. You're in the business of people's hopes and dreams.' So that was my very first lesson and it's everywhere now, people talk about it all the time, 'What's your purpose? What's your "Why?"?' All this shit you keep hearing. It's the latest and greatest, trendiest thing. Well, this was back in 1999, twenty-one years ago, and one of the best investors around, one of the most powerful people in Australia at the time, was asking me,

'Do you understand your purpose, your "Why?"?'

It was probably one of the most important questions and one of the most important lessons I ever got from 'the big dog', *ever*. It sort of irks me today that everybody is always talking about this idea, there's courses on it, people go to seminars to find out this shit. It's as if they've just discovered it. Kerry Packer knew about this a million years ago, which is probably why Channel 9 was so successful at the time. It was number one. It's why he knew people wanted World Series Cricket before they knew it themselves, and it was the reason why he wanted to invest in our business. Because he knew that the banks couldn't deliver the 'why' or 'the purpose', they couldn't deliver the message properly. He told me,

'Unless you understand your purpose – the
business you are actually in – then you can't
build a message and you can't market it.'

You just can't market it if you don't know the message and you can't build a message unless you know what the customer's purpose is. Not yours, *theirs*. It is the gospel truth. They're not after borrowing money, they don't want to borrow money from you! That means they've got to pay you back. They hate that. What they're looking at you for is someone to get them into their *dream*, their home, or their investment, or whatever it is that they're trying to do. It's something they've dreamt about. They're dreaming about security for the future, for investment portfolios. They're dreaming about a home for their family or just a roof over their heads. It's a basic entitlement that everybody believes they should have. The right to live in shelter, securely and safely. Now, more than ever, with recent devastating bushfires, seemingly endless droughts and the uncertainty of COVID-19, our basic safety and security is a real issue for us all.

So that was the first question and I'd come up empty-handed.

The second question was, no less tricky.

'Have you ever failed in business?'

I didn't realise the type of person Kerry Packer was. I didn't realise he was a counter-intuitive type of person. What you think he's wanting an answer for is not what he wants the answer for.

Counter-intuitive people are rare, the only other counter-intuitive person I had met prior to that was Rene Rivkin – the late Australian entrepreneur, stockbroker investor – and he was one of the smartest people I'd ever met. He was off the chart in terms of intellect, but had a few other issues as well that went against him in the long run. Rene was very counter-intuitive in the way he backed the markets. He bet against stocks and he was very successful in that regard.

Kerry was also counter-intuitive, so he would bet against the momentum and now he was asking me a question that was counter-intuitive. I immediately assumed, *Oh shit, he wants to hear that I've never failed, because why would he invest in me, someone who had failed before?*

In those days to be a failed entrepreneur was terrible, but today to be a failed entrepreneur is more like a badge of honour. Go to San Francisco, it's almost a requirement before venture capitalists invest in you – they want to know that you've gone out there, failed or nearly failed, and pivoted. They're looking at your ability to jink and twist and turn, and overcome difficulties. Because the reality is there's no such thing as a perfect run. Business is full of difficulties. Today, more than ever, we keep hearing about 'resilience'. Think hard on this:

'Resilience is the ability to fail, fail fast and
pivot and turn yourself into something else.'

So my response to Kerry's question was, 'No, I've never failed', because I hadn't ever failed in business. I mean, sure, I'd bought properties that might not have made as much money as expected, but I'd never really got caught in a property downturn. I'd been caught in share market downturns, but never in a business sense. I hadn't been in that many businesses either. It wasn't as if I was a serial businessman. I didn't have thirty businesses behind me because I was only in my early forties. I had been involved in professional environments, but not really as a businessman.

What he was trying to work out was, did I have the fortitude and the strength of character to change tack, because he was about to give me a whole lot of money. He said, 'What I don't want to happen is that I give you a whole lot of money and the moment one of your assumptions that you put in, or your modelling that we've done our due diligence on, doesn't come true, which is nine times out of ten. They're just assumptions on day one, by year three or four, or two even, those assumptions can be turned on their head completely.'

'The resilient people, the good quality people you want to invest in, and the successful people, what they tend to be able to do as a rule is to pivot or change tack broadly or even in a small way, but enough to guide themselves through the channels.'

He wanted to make sure that I had done this before. He was used to investing in start-up people all the time. That wasn't my game, I had been in professional business environments prior to this point.

No one had asked me that question before in the due diligence process. All anybody was interested in prior to that, all the professionals, was the modelling and looking at what was in existence in terms of the business. How was the business travelling relative to the modelling? Is the modelling relevant to how the facts are today? Are the forecasts relevant to the actuals? Do we need external analysis with investment bankers and various other experts on the mortgage market, the liquidity? I knew that stuff backwards, so I knew we were okay. I knew that in terms of sensitivity analysis and what I presented, even if you dropped my volumes down by 10 per cent or 20 per cent, I was still going to get a range of enterprise value that was acceptable to me and to them.

We were playing one of those games where there was never really going to be a failure between either me (the vendor) or Kerry Packer (the buyer). I knew that, he knew that too. Everybody I was talking to in the due diligence process was like me, we were all the same people. We were all just shit talkers basically. We talked in numbers, in formulas, and recipes and financial models. And we talked about what everyone else in the market talked about. We were all on a rising tide of liquidity, globally. No one was going to disagree with that. All Kerry wanted to know was that if something did happen, if something did change, then, 'How well prepared are you? What are you like? Because I'm going to give you my money. Are you going to fucking run away? Are you tough enough to hang in there or are you just going to walk?'

'He wanted to know that I would fight for it.'

That's what he was after. I didn't realise it at the time, but he really understood people's emotions and character. He was big on character and I'd never really dealt with someone like that before. I'd never come across anyone who was big on character in terms of being in business with you. 'What's your character like?' That was an important thing for him. Maybe because he was going through the big debacle that was One.Tel and there were a few other things going on that he didn't like. I don't know. Again, he was satisfied with the answer I gave because I told the truth, but I think he also thought, *I'd better keep my eye on this guy just in case, because he's never been tested.*

The third question was about accountability. It was interesting, to say the least.

The third question was the most important question that anyone could've asked and no one had asked it in the whole process.

It was actually an incredible question. I had assumed by then, because of his first question, that he hadn't read any of the paperwork. And he probably hadn't read it, but he would definitely have been briefed. He knew the questions to ask.

The third question wasn't a question per se, it was more a proposition.

My business at the time was as a reseller of other people's money. Somebody went out into the market and securitised money, the money was just like a white label product, it wasn't Westpac, ANZ or anything like that, it was just white label money and they allowed me to put my brand on it – Wizard – and sell it at my price. They would deliver me the money at a certain price, let's say they delivered me the money at 3 per cent, and then I was free to lend it at any price I wanted, but let's say I lent it at 4 per cent. The situation was that at that stage I was not manufacturing the money.

Kerry said to me, 'The entity that you're getting the money from – the entity that does the securitisation, manufactures the money – we need to buy a share in that entity. We can't just be a price taker for the rest of our lives.' He continued, 'Because what's going to happen is this: you'll build up your book of mortgages, and that entity who delivers the money to you, they might just say, "Our book is big enough now, we don't need any more, we're just going to milk you."'

He explained it to me using the example of how Warner Bros used to sell their programming in the TV world. He was familiar with this through Channel 9. Warner Bros was a program distributor in Australia, they didn't produce that much here themselves. Once or twice a year, Warner Bros went overseas and they bought whatever was available. I was doing the same thing, I was just buying money from one vendor and I was selling that one vendor's product. But what happens when you do that is you become totally reliant upon that entity, and they can really fuck you at any time if they want.

'We've got to buy an interest in that entity,' he said, 'or we've got to buy that entity or buy an influential interest in that entity because if that entity goes up in value and they want to do something wrong to us, we have a say, and/or if they're trying to profit off the back of what we've built, we're one of the ones that profit as well.' It's de-risking outcomes.

I had thought about that before, but it hadn't been a priority for me. I was enjoying sucking on the lolly. It was all going too well, but I knew in the back of my head that was something we should do.

He asked, 'Do you agree with that?'

'Yeah, I do.'

'I thought you'd say that.' And then he said, 'I'm going to have a side agreement with you. We won't write it up, but we've got to buy into the new entity, together, acquire an influential interest in that entity, or all of it, within the next twelve months. Do you agree with that?'

'I do. I agree, yeah.'

'Okay. You and me, we've got an agreement.'

I never thought about whether it was possible. What was I going to say? No? I had no choice; he knew I had no choice. I think he was testing me to see how I would go about it, what my response would be. His ability to control the situation was incredible. It was outrageously good. I was completely in awe of the situation I was in. I just couldn't believe it, he had me on a string, he was pulling me around wherever he wanted to pull me and I was always going to say yes, no matter what. Kerry Packer knew that. There was a cheque in front of me and an agreement, I wasn't going to say no. And it was logical. It made sense what he said. I did agree with him and I would've done it, but I would never have made it a priority.

Then he added this, 'Well, I'll tell you what. If you don't do that within twelve months, you give me all my money back, my twenty-five million. I'm investing twenty-five million in your company, to own fifty per cent of it, which we're going to use to build branches and all that stuff, we're going to do that. But in one year, if we don't own or don't have an influential interest in that business entity, you give me my twenty-five million back and I'll walk away, you'll walk away and you can own the company on your own. Do you agree to that?'

And I said, 'Yes.'

Firstly, I didn't know where I would get the $25 million from because I didn't have assets to access $25 million. Secondly, I didn't know if I could get the deal with the entity done, but I guess his third point and his due diligence in that meeting was to see where I would go.

I don't know what outcome he wanted me to go for, but he put himself in a position of no loss. Because the bottom line was if I failed to pay him back the $25 million, the first asset he would come after would be Wizard, because that's my asset. And he would then own 100 per cent of Wizard. So, there was no downside for him. He would go from owning 50 per cent for $25 million to 100 per cent for $25 million. Can you see the brilliance of that? I can. Or better still, if I didn't fail then we'd own half the other business, with his $25 million probably worth $50 million. Either way, he wouldn't lose.

Now, I don't know whether he sat up all night thinking about this, but my gut feeling is he was just working his way through it as he was going along. This all took hours, by the way. But that's my gut feeling. Because he was asking about the market and we were talking about a whole bunch of different things. I don't think he'd given it a minute's thought beforehand. I just think he was so experienced and so good, and so intuitive and so insightful, and he'd probably done this a hundred times before. And he was a great judge of character. At the start of our meeting, he didn't know me, so he was assessing me as he was going along, knowing the answers I would probably give, based on the berley he was leaving in front of me. He hooked me completely.

No wonder he was a good gambler. There was a gamble in that. I could have said no and walked out, but he knew that I wouldn't. It was just the most beautiful piece of business manoeuvring I've ever seen. There was no way out. It was a beautiful geometric shape. Euclid would have been proud of him.

I walked away thinking, *Sure, we've got $25 million in the account, but I've got a whole lot of work to do. I've got to make that $25 million sing. I've got to make things happen. I'm going to roll everything out. Plus, I've got to buy this fucking entity business or part of it.*

His view was, 'I'm going to invest in the business. I believe in the model. I like what you do, I'm going to support you. But I'm going to keep you accountable. I've got this thing in one year's time, but every month you come and see me. And you turn up and you tell me how the business is, how much money has gone into the business, how much has gone out of the business, how much we owe, what's in our bank account.' That's all he wanted to know except for one other question. 'How are you going with this deal?' Every month. Therein is a story itself.

•

Fast-forward twelve months. Kerry gave us incredible support and honoured everything we agreed on. But the pressure was on me. It got towards the end of the twelve months and I couldn't get the additional deal done because this entity was owned by a big Dutch bank and in Australia it was an entity of global significance in this particular market segment of Australian-backed mortgage securities.

Australian-backed mortgage bonds had been around for a long, long time, originally set up by AMP, then bought by BZW, an English investment bank. Then ABN AMRO bought it from them to have a presence here in Australia. ABN AMRO was the big Dutch bank. They were making money, good money. I was making it for them because I was placing their loans through my branches around Australia. And I was making money out of it, too. And so was Kerry. There was money in it for everybody. But they were making the lion's share of every mortgage.

The way the capital markets worked in those days was that interest rates went up for six months, then they would go down for six months, up for six months and down for six. That was the cycle. And, usually, interest rates went up five, six times, they'd plateau for a month or two, then they'd go down for five or six months. It's not like that now, it's different. But back then it was very predictable. And because it was so predictable, the wholesale company, ABN AMRO and their subsidiaries, could play with the capital markets and make money on the way up and make extra money on the way down.

The entity didn't want to sell. They didn't need to sell. But luckily, Wizard's agreement with them as their primary client was due to come to an end in six or seven months, towards the end of the twelve-month period that Kerry had given me. I was getting nowhere here in Australia, so I went overseas. It was a crazy thing to do, but I decided to fly to Amsterdam, go to the head office of this big bank and meet the chairman of the bank, or the CEO of the bank, the big Dutch dude. So, I just did that. I'd never been to Holland before, never been to Amsterdam. What the hell?

I don't know what inspired me to do it. Well, that's not true, but I'll reveal that story later.

I flew there, went to the head office and waited in reception. When I had mustered up enough guts – Dutch courage you might say – I went to the receptionist and said, 'I'm here to see Mr So-and-So,' whatever his name was. I'd looked him up, knew who he was.

She said, 'You don't have an appointment.'

'That's fine, I'll wait.'

I thought, *I'll just wait here in reception forever until I get a meeting with this guy.* I'll come back tomorrow if I have to and the next day and the day after that. I'll keep coming back because I've got to get this deal done and I'm not getting anywhere in Australia.

Eventually, the guy came down and asked me what I wanted. He didn't know who I was. The big boss of one of the biggest banks in Europe, one of the biggest banks in the world, and I'm just this no one from Australia.

I told him quickly what I was about and he invited me up to his office. We talked, he said he would come to Australia on his next Asian-Pacific visit and he said he would go and see Kerry Packer.

I thought, *Fuck.* That was not what I wanted to happen. I've got to do the deal, not Kerry.

I didn't make the twelve-month deadline. Kerry called me and tried to get me to go in and see him. I was working on a deal with a German bank, Deutsche Bank, or their subsidiary here, which ran a big fund for superannuation funds. I was trying to bring them in as a one-third partner as well because they had approached me and my brother and so we were working on the deal. Kerry asked me how the Dutch bank deal was going, and I said, 'Well, I don't know. I'm in the middle of due diligence with this German bank.' He was aware of that. I said, 'I need time.' So, I just avoided his calls for a few months. 'Sorry, I can't, I'm too busy.' And I'm talking to someone who is really busy, like he's going, 'Get here. I needed this to happen on the twelve-month anniversary of the day you signed the agreement originally.' I bought myself another couple of months and, in that period, I agreed in principle to a deal with Deutsche Bank, to invest more money into Wizard for one-third.

Kerry, at that stage, had not approved them coming in at all because if it happened it meant that his share would have gone down to one-third. I'm one-third, he's one-third and they're one-third. But they were going to put a lot of money into the business, like $60 million. A huge amount of money. And we could do a lot of stuff for them, but most importantly, I thought we could buy out the Dutch bank, that we could buy their part of the wholesale business here.

The Dutch banker did come to Sydney as he said he would and he did meet with Kerry. Kerry rang me, and said, 'Come and see me. You've got a deal. The Dutch will sell forty-nine per cent of that entity here in Australia. Well done.' He went on, 'The bloke told me you'd gone to see him.' So, we worked out the price, started working with their lawyers and then I went back and I told him the price, and he said to me, 'How much money do you think we need? How much money do we need to buy the Dutch guy out?'

The evaluation was $25 million. We needed $12.5 million to buy half, forty-nine per cent. And he asked, 'Do we need integration money?' At this stage, I hadn't done the deal with the Germans, it wasn't finalised. He said, 'The price is probably about five million to do the integration.' So that's like seventeen to eighteen million bucks we needed, but we didn't have enough money in the bank. So he reached down, pulled his cheque book out, and started writing a cheque.

He said, 'We're going to need money, aren't we?'

'Yeah,' I said. 'We're going to need ten million bucks.'

He started writing a cheque for five million dollars, and he said, 'Wizard Home Loans, five million dollars.'

And I said, 'Okay. I was thinking, probably that would be ten million.'

'Well,' he said, 'you've got until Friday to put your five in.'

I didn't have five million dollars lying around. I said, 'I'm forty-three years of age, what the fuck's wrong with you? I've put everything into this.'

'Well, if you don't put the money in,' he said, 'I'm going to dilute you.'

I'm thinking, *I've just done the thing you told me to do?* Maybe he was setting me up to not do the deal all along so that he could get the whole thing for $25 million. He's set me up to dilute me from 50 per cent down to some other number, which would give him the majority interest. Even if I went down to 49 per cent he'd own it, because 51 per cent means he's got it. I'm fucked because no one's going to buy me as a minority interest.

My brother was at ING Bank at the time. I told him where things were at and he went out and closed the deal with Deutsche Bank. They invested, we had a deal on the table now for them to invest $60 million into Wizard.

I went back to Kerry, and said, 'Here's your fucking five million back,' and gave him his cheque. 'I'm going to put a cheque in for sixty million. We're going to bank sixty million, we're going to buy half of the Dutch bank's business here in Australia and we're going to have a whole lot more money left in the bank.'

'Well, hang on,' he said. 'What does that mean?'

I said, 'We're going to give them a third.'

'I don't do thirds,' he said. 'I own one hundred per cent. I want to control these things.'

'What's bothering you?' I asked.

'Well, they might outvote me.'

'How can they? They'd have to get me on side for that. We'd have to vote against you.' Me, a third, them, a third, against your third. 'So why don't you and I just sign an agreement that we'll always vote on the same lines, party lines. Exactly the same. And I'll never deviate from that. You can sue me if I do. We'll always outvote them. You've gone from fifty per cent to sixty-six per cent now.'

'I like that,' he said. 'Deal.'

So, we did a deal.

•

Now, I had had time to think about all these things. I had thought this through, but the way Kerry Packer positioned me, I'm sure he didn't think it through. As I said earlier, I'm sure he just did it off the cuff. His positioning of me was nothing short of brilliant because of that. Me, I had to have plenty of time to think about how to get anywhere near him. I had like a year, fifteen months to plan.

But we ended up with $60 million in the bank and owned half of the Dutch bank subsidiary here. Kerry and I controlled the business with 66 per cent and always voted on the same lines. We had a German bank, Deutsche Bank, as our partner.

Things always change though. You can never stay still in business or you lose eventually. The moment we got control of this subsidiary entity, it needed a warehouse alliance. The way these things work is you've got to have a warehouse alliance; it means that the banking sector gives the subsidiary entity, the securitisation entity, a billion dollars here and a billion dollars there, and you go out and you lend it to Australians to buy homes. And then, what you do is you bundle all those up into bonds and you sell them into the bond market and you refresh your position. You pay back the bank and start all over again. It's just like a line of credit for a billion dollars at a time, and Deutsche Bank was one of the lines of credit. They liked that. They were our American conduit to the market, which was really important.

ABN AMRO was our European contract to the market, so we raised money in both Europe and America. Eventually, Wizard bought 100 per cent of the subsidiary. We bought the other 50 per cent and we gave ABN AMRO some cash and stock in Wizard. ABN AMRO became a quarter shareholder, Kerry and I were 50 per cent and Deutsche Bank was 25 per cent. I had no idea it was going to be that big, but the only way it became so big was because Kerry made that agreement with me that I had to buy into that entity. And the only way we were going to be able to buy it was if I got more funding. The only way I was going to get more funding was to let someone else in as a shareholder. I was never going to be able to buy the Dutch out, they wanted to have some equity in the business.

On my board, I had someone from Deutsche Bank, someone from ABN AMRO, someone from Packer, and me. So, we had a pretty heavy board at Wizard. We owned the biggest issue of Australian-backed mortgage bonds in the world, that was part of our group. It was a company called AMS, Australian Mortgage Securities. We ran the biggest, mortgage-backed bond platform in the world, a thing called the ARMS II program – Australian Residential Mortgage Securities II program – and we ran it like a bank. I mean, we had two banks as our shareholders and we ran this like a bank. We had asset liability committees. We had to manage the liquidity to make sure that we always had enough money in the warehouses to lend to the demand from Australians and from our branches, and from other people. We ended up white labelling other lenders as well. And so, it was like a juggling act. And then every six, seven weeks, I would go overseas with Deutsche Bank and ABN AMRO, and we'd issue bonds, we'd refresh our warehouses and away we'd go again. That was the business. So, eventually, I was able to use my master's degree in capital markets. That's the part of the business that I ran.

And it all came off the back of Kerry Packer giving me one proposition in one meeting.

How would you know that something like that was going to happen? I could never work that out. Circumstances, opportunism, pressure, survival. The trip to Amsterdam was pretty important. That was a gutsy thing to do. Earlier I said that I didn't know what made me do it. That's not true. I'll tell you something about that, something really important.

The parable of the Yugoslav excavator

I have a friend, Bill Shipton, and Bill and I had this building company many years before Wizard. We used to do developments, little developments. We'd buy a house and land package site, and we'd build up houses and sell them off. We never really made any money, but Bill was a very successful builder.

Bill told me this story once, and I'll never forget it. Bill had a guy who worked for him, an excavator. I met him. Big, tall Yugoslav guy. He was a scary-looking dude, like most excavators and demolishers in those days. I don't know about these days, but back then they looked like they could do just about anything. They've got to demolish a building, who knows where they dumped it? Who would know?

I can't remember the Yugoslav excavator's name, but he claimed Bill owed him some money for a job. There was a dispute as to how much it was. Now, Bill was a really tough sort of guy himself, like no backward steps. He was a pretty fearless sort of bloke and he wasn't going to just let this one slide. But this excavator used to turn up to Bill's office and just sit in the reception. He'd say, 'I want to see Bill,' and would stand there or sit down if there was a seat, day after day. And Bill would be in his office like, 'What the fuck? What am I going to do? This guy's sitting there, says I owe him money. He's still sitting there. I've got to deal with him. Just sitting in my office every day, just turning up and waiting.' And Bill said it was quite intimidating. Half of that was because the guy was a big, tall Yugoslav mad bastard.

That story struck a chord with me and I remembered it when I was dealing with the Dutch bank. Not that I wanted to intimidate the guy from the Dutch bank, but I thought, *That works, it does*. That basic shit works. I knew it worked with Bill – because he ended up paying – but I thought I'd try it too.

'Sometimes, you've just got to go back to fundamentals.'

It's true. Sometimes you have to go back to basics to cut through the bullshit. Especially when you've got the sword of Damocles or Kerry Packer hanging over your head. And for me, it was all or nothing with Kerry. It was always going to be everything's going to be great or nothing's going to be great with the thought that he could come and collect the whole thing off me. Kerry taught me a lot in business chess. I learned by observing him, observing the way he was. I can't be like him, but I did learn stuff from him.

•

I had a good friendship with Kerry. I wasn't his best mate or anything, but we had a good relationship and we were doing well in business. We were a good asset for him, one of his better-performing assets. He bought into a lot of businesses, like clothing businesses, where he got dudded, and One.Tel where he got smashed. Not us though. We did everything we said we would do, *everything*. And I was transparent. People talk about mentors – he wasn't my mentor, he never offered to be my mentor and I never asked him to be my mentor, I didn't even know what a mentor was in those days. But he acted like a mentor in that he kept me accountable and he asked me questions.

He'd ask me a question, I'd deliver an answer and he'd hold me to it. That's it. To me, the whole premise of mentoring is about that. I'm not here to give you advice. You tell me what's going on, brief me. I'll ask you some questions, you give me some answers and then take the answers and do with them what you want. Because they're your answers. They're not my answers.

I can't tell you how to run a delicatessen. I can ask you some questions about your deli and I'll try to be like Kerry and drill down to the important things, like he did in my business, the supply and money. Liquidity is the most important thing. He said to me, 'Listen, I don't know how well you advertise in the market, whether you've got ten thousand enquiries or not. I don't care how good you are at that other stuff, but you've got to have liquidity, the money's got to be flowing through to service your customers.' It was the same at Channel 9. If Channel 9 couldn't get the programs, it didn't matter how many people wanted to watch Channel 9, they'd start dropping off. Which is what happened when Foxtel arrived because Foxtel just offered more programming. There was nothing Channel 9 could do about that, zero.

That was the end of Channel 9 in terms of being worth billions of dollars. It's still worth something, but it went down from that period. And I think he sort of knew that stuff. It was Kerry who encouraged me to sell the business to General Electric. Or at least to sell it because he was worried about global liquidity in 2004.

The GFC happened in 2008, but he was worried about it in 2004. He was worried about the ability of the banking system to live up to the various promises that they make. In our case, we borrowed all our money through this subsidiary of the Dutch bank we'd bought. We borrowed all that money, or raised all that money, through bond issuance in America and Europe. A little bit in Australia, but not much. It was a very shallow market here, not enough liquidity or depth for the sort of levels of money that we needed. And everyone, all of us, were competing with the banks, we were all doing the same thing.

In those days, 60 per cent of all money lent to Australians to buy houses came from capital markets. And of that 60 per cent, 95 per cent of it came from overseas capital markets. That's from all banks. It wasn't coming from the depositors, it wasn't coming from you putting your money in the banks. There aren't enough depositors, not enough people to save money. What happens when you borrow or when you raise this money? If you raise it in America, Europe or the UK they'll give you the money in their currency – US dollars, euros and pound sterling – and they expect you to pay it back in their currency, so you have currency risk. Then they pay you, and you agree to pay them an interest rate. If you're borrowing in US dollars, you pay a US dollar interest rate, which is quite low. But those interest rates move up and down, which you have no control of. Same as if I'm borrowing pound sterling or euros, I'm paying sterling interest rates or European interest rates, whatever the reserve bank there or whatever the Chancellor of the Exchequer says the interest rate's going to be. And then they expect you to not only pay them back, but pay them back their principal based on an agreement. But your borrower, my borrower here in Australia, might say, 'No, I want to pay my loan off faster.'

●

In Australia people love real estate and all the bond holders around the world had a massive appetite for our stuff. They would ring me up from America and would be saying, 'Look, can we buy $500 million worth of mortgages?' There was massive demand for our stuff because Australian-backed mortgages, not just ours, but anything coming out of Australia, was sought after around the world. Everybody wanted to own Australian-backed mortgage bonds because Australian mortgages were performing the best in the world. And that's still the case today. They were a highly sought after asset class around the world and all the big super funds around the world all die for this stuff. All the big hedge funds, they all wanted part of it. They couldn't get enough of it.

There weren't that many issuers. We were one of them. We were the biggest. I thought nothing would stop it. I thought, *Well, what's going to stop it?* It's a bit like someone saying today, 'The interest rates might go up.' What's going to put the interest rates up? Well, they will go up, I can guarantee it. But we just don't know what it is that will make them go up. Just like with the GFC. What was going to cause a problem? No one knew it was going to be the GFC, just like no one knew COVID-19 was going to hit. Something always happens every ten years. You don't know what it is but some shit always happens and Kerry knew that, because he said, 'Well, maybe it's time to think about selling out.'

•

I used to pick Kerry up whenever the Sydney Roosters played at home. I would go to his house, pick him up and take him to the game.

I used to have a bet, or he'd have a bet with me between ourselves. He hated the Roosters, he just liked to see us lose, but that was okay.

I'd drop him off and sometimes stay to have something to eat after navigating my way past the rottweilers that he used to have, which terrified me. I had a good relationship with him, and with James. There was a lot of discussion around at the time, 'Are you a mate of James or a mate of Kerry?' An MOJ or an MOK. It was in the newspapers. I mean, the *Financial Review* wrote a big article about it once and they said I was an MOK, a mate of Kerry, as opposed to a mate of James. I was a mate of both, which doesn't make as good newspaper copy.

Two or three weeks before Christmas 2005, Kerry invited me to go away with him to Tahiti on his boat on Christmas Day.

I wanted to stay in Australia to see my kids so I said, 'No, I want to see my kids and family.'

'Come on,' he said. 'Meet me and we'll fly over. Or come over after.'

I didn't go.

He passed away on Boxing Day.

ASK YOURSELF THE THREE QUESTIONS
KERRY PACKER ASKED ME

1. What business are you in?

2. Have you ever failed?

3. Do you consider yourself resilient?

Answer truthfully and consider what your answers say about you.

Think for Yourself

Stop worrying about things you can't control

At the moment we're all getting sucked into constantly paying attention to the media. The media wants everybody to listen to what they've got to say and follow them because they sell advertising, by eyeballs. You need to know what's going on once a day or once a week maybe. You don't need to sit there looking at the news for twenty hours a day and you don't need to feel the way they want you to feel. They want you to feel scared. There's no need to feel scared.

'Start to think for yourself.'

You're creative. Think about what you have got to do with your business right now so that when things change you can emerge ahead of everybody else. Have I got to build my brand? Do I need to build my inventory, build my systems? Should I build my relationships with my colleagues, my staff, my contractors? Have I got to pivot my product or my service? Where is the demand, what do people want? Just keep asking those questions of yourself every day instead of sitting there listening to what you are being fed. Stop thinking about shit you can't control. Just think about what you can do.

No matter what the latest crisis is (and there will be one) minimise how much you tap into the news cycle. It is exhausting and takes your energy away from the things that really matter. Rather than disappear into the social media black hole and read posts on Twitter all day, stop talking about it. It's wasting your energy. You're better off spending time with your mum or your dad or your kids, getting on a bike or going for a run, rather than thinking about that shit. You can find out all you need to, in terms of news, once a day.

What happened to old-fashioned gratitude?

What happened to our ability to see the good in life? More and more I notice people's utter lack of gratitude these days. Instead of feeling grateful many people feel compelled to argue for the sake of it, to criticise based on political lines, or to just bag the shit out of those who have stood up for the job of running this country. Are we really that desperate for some relevance?

The media have taken it upon themselves to be the arbiter of all common sense and to tell us what is right. Where is their mandate? What's their agenda? Did you vote for them? I know I certainly didn't. 'News' doesn't have to be negative. The process should remain that if we don't like what a party has put into place then we vote them out. But let's not disrespectfully harangue and put politicians out to dry after we voted them in.

Let's debate and discuss the important issues like adults, but let's do it with a bit more old-fashioned respect and gratitude.

Hard times

I mentioned earlier that *Being There* is one of my favourite films, the other is another movie from the 1970s called *Hard Times*. It's set during the Great Depression and stars Charles Bronson as a bare-knuckle boxer trying to survive and James Coburn as his slick and wasteful promoter.

For anyone in business, especially right now, I recommend hunting it down and watching it. There are some great parallels and lessons for the business owner.

What I loved about the movie is embodied in the main character. It comes down to two things: the idea of a fighter and the fact that content is important. Charles Bronson represented the content that the James Coburn character, the promoter, needed, but his content was never actually valued. Coburn was not respectful of the content until right at the very end. He was gambling with Charles Bronson's character's ability to fight, his willingness to fight.

Let's talk about the content. The content was not only Charles Bronson's skill and his toughness, it was also his willingness. Not many people would be prepared to put themselves through that shit, for a very small amount of money, just enough to survive. For me, it epitomises what happens in business all the time.

I rely on the media to promote my business, because if I don't have the media, no one's going to come to me. No one will join me at one of my outlets at Wizard or Yellow Brick Road. To some extent, I'm just content for the media and what I didn't realise at first is that I thought I was more important than I really was. In the movie, Charles Bronson's character knew all along what he was. He was just there to be played with and, as long as you accept that position, you're okay. The moment you don't accept that position and think that you're actually important, that's when you're going to be really disappointed in the way you're treated.

I've been through that process. I've experienced being a darling of the media, and I used the media to promote myself. Anyone who's trying to build a brand uses modern-day media platforms, but then they start complaining when they get trolled or they start complaining when people don't like them as much or they start complaining about how hard it is, how much time and effort they've got to put into it. When I was younger I used to get troubled by that too.

In the movie, Charles Bronson's character never complained once, he knew exactly what the deal was. Today, like Bronson, I know exactly what the deal is.

The James Coburn character is just promoting someone else's story, that's all he's doing to make money, and the media's the same. I used the media just like Charles Bronson's character did to find me the people 'to fight'. The media used to use me as a matchmaker and I'd often be disappointed because the media would do and say things that I'd think were inappropriate. Over time I realised that's the game. And it is no different from what James Coburn was doing to Charles Bronson in the movie.

Mike Tyson says you don't know what it's like until you get punched in the face. Most people get on media platforms and they say all sorts of things, they rip into people. You can say whatever you like, but when you get punched in the face, you know that you've got to stop or that's the penalty, the punishment, you're going to get.

In *Hard Times*, Charles Bronson's character never seemed to doubt his ability going into any of the fights. Well, that's how it seemed and that's how I like to present myself, even when I go into the boxing ring. I'm the same in business.

When I started Wizard, I felt like I was the loner coming into town just like the lead character in *Hard Times*. I rode into town looking to take on everybody. Fight the odds.

We used to love that idea in Australia. We Australians loved the underdog who was up for the fight. But, it seems to me, somewhere along the way we've lost our collective willingness to fight

We've got to stop. No one's questioning some of the politicians at the moment, no one's taking them to task. Why? I am not talking about trolling them, I am talking about holding them to scrutiny and making them answer questions. Transparency in government has diminished and we need to bring that back so we can assess if politicians are doing the right thing by us or not.

No one takes the banks to task anymore either. No one questions anything anymore and I think we've lost that fight here in Australia. Charles Bronson's character questioned the conventional wisdom that everyone was going to beat him.

At the end of the movie, Charles Bronson's character is done for that transaction – fighting in New Orleans – but that's not his last transaction, he'll transact again wherever he's going, that's what I read from it. He's just getting on the train going to the next station or the next place and he'll transact again if he wants to, if he feels inspired to or if he needs to. He'll go again and why not?

What I did at Wizard – building the business, the whole thing – was a transaction. I don't mean I did it to make a profit or to sell it, it was just a transaction in my life. I did another one, Yellow Brick Broad, and then another one, Mentored, and I'll do another one after that, I hope. I don't want too much, I'm not trying to take money from everybody, I'm happy for everybody to get their share. But this is what I do.

I wouldn't say that I don't always have extended agendas, sometimes I do. But none of them are going to be at anyone else's expense. I just don't do that. I don't trade at other people's expense, ever. It's a principle of mine, a standard of mine. Some people think that I'm always up to something, but I'm not. I actually am doing what I'm doing, there's no extra agenda.

We're in hard times at the moment, as I write this we are in the worst recession since the Great Depression. That's really important and it's what you get from Charles Bronson in *Hard Times*.

> 'You've gotta be fuckin' tough. You've gotta fuckin' stand up. You wanna take on all the big guys? Then be prepared to stand up to them. Fight 'em, no matter what, no matter what. If you're going to get beaten up, so be it. Be prepared for that.'

Don't go thinking, *Shit, I can't do this*. It's all about survival. Once you're in it, you've got to learn how to survive. Act like a survivor – feel like Charles Bronson and think like a simpleton – be like Peter Sellers in *Being There*.

> 'Change your state of mind, do something.'

Fight the battles that matter most

Only fight one or two battles at a time. Don't create drama for yourself when you don't need to. I know people who create so many little skirmishes that rob them of focus and energy when there's a big war coming towards them. What are you doing? Why would you do that? I say to my team all the time, 'Listen, we've got something coming towards us, I'm not interested in all that other shit. I don't need to have the internal battles, I don't need to have dramas here, dramas over there.'

I had a meeting recently with my team and they said there was something they wanted to do and I said, 'There's no need to do that, it's just going to cause a battle, a small battle, we'll win it but there's nothing in it for us, there's no point.' It was a principle thing for them. I said, 'I don't care about the principle, we just go on with it for the time being. It doesn't matter. It's not hurting us if we can manage it. We've got something else we want to do over here, that's more important for me.'

When I talk about battles, I don't mean battles in the military sense, it's maybe strategic moves. It might be a takeover or it might be an asset you're trying to buy and these 'battles' could purely be strategies, both offensive and defensive. Not aggressive, not necessarily an attack. It could be in relation to a competitor. We are having battles with our competitors in an unusual sense every day. We are always competing with our competitor for 'the real estate'. In business, it's about the precious real estate of people's minds – someone's view of you as a brand.

Or the real estate could be market share, the market for mortgages. So, I'm in a battle with everyone else for that market share. It could be a reducing market share, mortgages have been getting less amounts and there are less of them, which is the case at the moment. The battle is me beating everybody else to that market share. That's the real estate I'm after.

'What's the real estate you're after?'

Battles in many ways can also be relationships, chasing resources or defending the resources you have against somebody else who wants your resources. One way to get someone's market share, one way to get real estate, is to go and take someone else's away from them. Not competing with what's out there in the marketplace but taking my real estate away from me. So, if someone wants to take over my company, they're not competing with me for market share, they're actually coming to take my market share, take it away from me altogether.

Pay attention to feedback but don't make it your true north

If I get feedback I'll read it or I'll listen to it, but that's it. I don't go around encouraging it. I don't read anything about any of my TV shows. I used to, I don't anymore. The feedback people give me tends to be on social media and sometimes I'll read it, I'll look at it. I think about it for a minute, a few seconds, but normally I'll just dismiss it.

Some people might say I'm intellectually arrogant in that regard, that I have an arrogance about me. No, I just don't want to get bogged down in all that stuff.

Look at feedback, think about it and take it in. Whether you do something about it or not is up to you. Don't sit around with hundreds of advisors, like *Game of Thrones* where someone's in your ear all the time trying to manipulate you. It doesn't work.

Work together for common goals

I think we're going to go through a period, a year, after COVID-19 of trying to re-establish our commonality. I think we're going to experience a breakdown in relationships between states and within states. We're going to have these breakdowns for a period of time, until we can build some momentum back the other way about what matters, what's important. We'll probably get back to really basic stuff. Like just being able to go to the gym, to the park, being able to drive your car after a certain time at night, being able to visit grandparents and parents. I think we're going to go through a process of actually appreciating the fundamentals. That's not a bad thing.

To some extent, we've moved away from valuing the fundamentals. Of travel overseas, of travel interstate, travel within your five-kilometre radius, going to work, having a job, having a mortgage. They're all gold today. Having a mortgage is gold, because they're really hard to get. Owning a home. Having a job that supports your mortgage. Being able to pay the mortgage as opposed to asking for some sort of relief from your lender. I really think a new appreciation of those fundamentals – having a mum, being able to go and visit your dad – is on the way. During lockdown I couldn't go and visit my dad because it was too far to travel. Now I see him every Saturday, no matter what. The rules have been lifted and I have a new appreciation for what is important to me. I think our society is just starting to work out what fundamentals are important.

Cleanliness is important. Cleanliness of what you touch, cleanliness of what you eat, cleanliness of what you drink, who you mingle with or talk to. Why? Because you might bring COVID-19 home and give it to your father, or your son or daughter, or your partner or your colleagues at work. They're the things we never thought about before and these fundamentals are really important. We haven't really got them set down yet. We're just realising the fundamentals now, the fundamentals of an economy.

In recent years, we've always grown as a country economically. I think we are the only country in the world that grew for seventy-five quarters or something like that, without a hiccup. This is the first time that we haven't grown, so most people in this country – most young people and a lot of middle-aged people – have never seen a recession. We just took growth for granted. Our business would grow, our revenue would grow, our income's going to grow, my house value's going to grow, my superannuation's going to grow. We've lived for so long in a growth environment in this country.

That's not going to be the case anymore. Some of us will grow and achieve, some will not. Some of us are going to go backwards. Super's going to go backwards, our income's going to go backwards, our house value's going to go backwards. Any combination or all of them. That's something we've never really experienced before. That's going to be a new fundamental.

'How are we going to deal with this
next period as a nation?'

Well, we're going to have a period of disappointment, shock, disillusionment, confusion. 'What am I going to do now?' I am already seeing it, people are reaching out to me all the time, 'What do I do?' This takes us right back to divergent thinking and *Being There*.

> 'Change your state of mind. Things
> aren't that bad for us.'

Life is not all about growth, in terms of assets, it's not just about that.

Are all Australians on the same page?

No. I think there's a whole middle section of Australians who're just not thinking about what's going on. They're just hoping that everything's going to be okay, just going about their business. Then there's the edges, both edges who are dictated to by the media, the left and the right, the two on the edge. The big piece in the middle, they don't quite know what effect this is going to have on them, they're not really feeling it just yet. They will. They will feel it next year.

This is the fiscal cliff everyone keeps talking about. I think it's going to be the recession that will be our third quarter of recession and there's always flow-on effects of this and the last bit to get affected is the middle section. There's one end of the marketplace that's going to make a lot of money, all the digital companies and technology, they're just going to make more and more money.

Then there's the other end, which are the retail shops, they're going to get hurt badly because the digital people want this to happen, because they want to take them out of the game. People with five or six restaurants have been hit by lockdowns and now with diminished numbers allowed in premises. That is going to hurt.

I think some of our political leaders are drinking from the cup of control. My gut feeling is they will survive between here and mid next year because they're going to scare the bejesus out of everybody and they're also going to present themselves as the saviours. But the thing that they haven't provided for is the economic downturn and they're not in control of that. The states are in control of protecting you from getting sick, running the trams and the buses and the hospitals and the universities, overseeing the gatherings and the police, so they can control the health outcomes. But they can't control the economic outcomes. That's outside their control, that's federal and they will eventually get blamed.

Can they come up with a solution? Our federal government only has to come up with a strategy that voters believe will work in the immediate future and they'll vote for them. The next federal election at the time of writing is in one and a half years or so, and for the federal government, the economic downturn will be best if it's around December next year. Then they just have to convince us that they're the solution to the problem. But the issue is, no one seems to think long term anymore. We need strategy, we need vision, we need divergent thinking. We need to back ourselves and get back to basics to change our future.

GET THROUGH HARD TIMES

1. Prepare for the hard times during the good times.
2. Only concern yourself with what you can control.
3. Don't lose yourself in a news and social media overload. Save your energy and free up your mind from the bombardment of a 24-hour news cycle.
4. Be grateful for what you have.
5. Pick your battles. Only fight if it will benefit you.
6. Don't let others define you – listen to feedback but only take onboard what you believe is right.

There's Always Another Fight

I always say, know who your buyer is. General Electric was the most obvious buyer to sell Wizard to. The only reason I said that is because I knew GE was the world's largest consumer lender in the world at the time and had big operations here in Australia. No one knew who they were. They were always under different names and things like that. They owned a mortgage insurance company here, and we were their biggest customer. I knew that if we sold our business to one of the banks, GE's insurance company would lose our business and I knew they wouldn't want that to happen. But at the same time, the Packer family owned a business here, which was run by James, called Challenger. When James Packer knew we were for sale, he wanted to buy the Wizard business and put it into Challenger. However, he wanted to make me part of Challenger. I would have had to stay on and I really didn't want to do that in a company and a culture I didn't know. Because Wizard would be part of them, not the other way around. I wanted to sell out completely and that's why GE became the most obvious buyer for me.

Kerry didn't do it, my brother and I, we got to GE, found the buyer, and then there was a seven-month period of negotiation and again, my brother just pushed really hard on that. As usual, he got the deal done. I agree to the deal, he stitches it up all the way through. I cut and he sewed. He acted for all of us: Deutsche Bank, ABN AMRO, Kerry Packer and me. He did the deal for everybody. That was it, it was June 2004, and the deal was done. I stayed close to Kerry after that, we didn't do anything else together before he died, but James and I would.

GE continued as Wizard and I was kept on as the Australian chairman. I stayed on because GE asked me to. They thought they needed me in the business because I built it. Sometimes you can't just walk away.

•

That was a great part of my life. Was I proud of myself? Yeah. Things were happening that had never happened to me before. I was on television and doing things like that. Did it go to my head? Probably a little bit in a relative sense, but compared to other people? No. Did I go out partying all the time? No. Not because I'm some kind of saint. It just didn't enter my head.

I probably had a bit of an ego at the time because I was hanging out with the Packers and other people like them so there was a bit of that, but I'm still a pretty down-to-earth bloke and, I have to be honest with you, those people who I was hanging out with, they're all pretty down-to-earth too. Everyone goes, 'Oh, James Packer,' but he was really young at the time, maybe thirty-something. David Gyngell was the same age, a bit older maybe. There was a group of them and they were all in their thirties, and there was no real ego there. Maybe a little bit, a little bit of privilege around them, but not too much.

I still used to see my older mates occasionally. Like I said, I'm not really a social guy, that's not my thing. So, I might have gone to an event like a wedding but I'm not the social type. Other people would meet up overseas, they would go skiing. I'm not a skier. I didn't do all that sort of stuff. I wasn't interested.

I sucked it up a little bit though. Probably enjoyed it a bit. I met some interesting people. I saw some interesting lifestyles, but it didn't take me long to work out what suited me, what didn't suit me, what I was comfortable with and not comfortable with.

My family didn't see much of me. That was a downside. I worked long, long hours, but I always made it my business to watch my sons' sporting events on weekends. Weekends were sacred for me. I have four sons, so Saturday was pretty much footy all day and Sunday was the same. They played union and league, as well as basketball, and did swimming too. A lot of times they had sport on Friday nights so I always made sure that I was there on Friday nights, available to go to their sport. I didn't take them to training very much, but I always attended their sport on weekends.

During the week they didn't see that much of me. I would always get home late; I didn't help them with their schoolwork and stuff like that. I wasn't there to ask, 'Have you done your homework?' or 'Can I help you with your homework?' I was always gone in the morning before they got up. So if you ask them, they would say I didn't spend a lot of time with my family.

I wasn't mature. Even at forty, I was still immature. I'm prepared to admit that. And I probably wasn't mindful of what my wife would be thinking. I didn't consider for one minute, 'Oh, I wonder what my wife thinks?' or 'What should I be doing to make her feel comfortable?'

I never thought of that. I just assumed she was fine. Everything was fine. You know, the money comes in the door, the kids are going to good schools. She's got three children and one from my previous marriage, four kids all together. The boys all love each other and they love their mother. We all get together on Christmas Day, we get together over Easter, we go to my parents' place, we all go on holidays. No one's ill. For me that was it, that was a perfect life.

I thought I had a perfect life. But then, obviously I didn't. I thought I had the perfect wife, the perfect family.

If something went wrong, then I would put it down to my not being aware of the impact of who I was seen as, as opposed to who I really was, because who you're seen as, I think, in a personal partnership sense, is pretty bloody important. Equally important, for the success of a business, is that you're seen in a certain way.

'You end up torn between them.'

That's what I had to do, I had to be seen in a certain way. I didn't create that, the media did that.

'I never sat down at any time in life and said,
I need to be seen as this particular person.'

I had decided to spend my time intellectually thinking about how to raise money. How was I going to get the next bond issue away? Because we were getting so many enquiries, we had to make sure we could fund it. I was conscious I had to look a certain way and all that sort of stuff, but I never really thought it through.

'Everyone thinks I'm some sort of
marketing guy. I am not.'

I'm not like John Symond. John is a marketing guru. What he did with the strapline of his business – 'We'll save you' – was brilliant. And the way he came across, his voice, everything. But that was all structured, that was all a well-oiled machine. My approach was very different, it was the tactical thing. We had the product, we had the system, we had the representation, we had all the other stuff going on, and it just worked. And I put all my energy and focus into the business. I never thought about it, but it put undue pressure on my then wife. And I think probably today my boys would say that, to some extent, it shaped who they are – in some negative ways and in some positive ways. That's my lot and my life and I have gratitude for so much but there are some things I think I could have done differently. Maturity has given me that widened perspective.

253

•

When I settled the deal with GE – GE paid me in GE shares – I had to collect my script in New York. There was no way in the world I was going to let them put it in an envelope and send it to me. I wanted to be there, at their office, collecting it. The settlement was happening in Australian time, which was 11 pm New York time.

I'd probably only been to New York once in my life before then. I booked into the Four Seasons Hotel, which I would not ordinarily stay in because it was expensive, and I walked down to this custodian building with a guy who was a custodian of GE shares. It was a bank in New York, and the guy had instructions to open up for me at a certain time. He got the okay which said, 'Yes, the transaction is completed and you can now issue Mark his shares.' I stood there and collected a big chunk of shares, one certificate, but worth a lot of money. I remember he put it in an envelope and I said, 'Thank you.' I walked out of this custodian office, walked back to the Four Seasons in New York at midnight, and it was like a total anticlimax for me.

I went back to my room and I was on my own. I ordered pizza, watched television, had a whisky, ate half the pizza and went to sleep. In the end I thought, *What the hell? What is that? What does it mean? Does it mean anything?*

It meant nothing. That sounds really bad. I don't want it to sound disrespectful but I thought, *What the fuck? It's just a piece of paper.*

All the years, all this time and effort and hard work and everything I'd done and all the thoughts I put into this business was reflected on one piece of paper. What is the meaning of that? It was a significant reflective time in my life. I turned the light off and went to sleep. I went to sleep happy, but no happier than I had been at a previous time.

Getting there

I know I've already talked a bit about *Being There*, one of my two favourite films, but what about the idea of 'getting there'?

The real buzz is not the end point, it's not where you land and all the things you buy and surround yourself with. It's about the process of getting there. My dream garage is to have a garage where I don't feel compelled to put anything in it. Material things tend to indicate success, in other words they're an affirmation to ourselves that we've done something really good. Most of the successful people I know – and especially the ones I've known in the past – don't have fancy cars, they don't walk around dreaming about a particular car and I think mainly the reason for that – and I've been through it myself, I've had all those cars – is you get to a point in your life where it's about practicality. You don't have to wear your successes on your sleeve, you don't have to wear them on your body, you don't have to display them to anybody for affirmation because you know what you've done.

'It's about your actions, it's not about your possessions.'

Sure, have a good car, a high quality car, a practical car, a car that speaks to the environment if that's important to you, have a car that has some luxury in it, but at the same time, you don't have to be pitching all your life towards getting this great outcome. The funny thing is, when you get to the great outcome you usually don't decide to spend your money on what you've been dreaming of. You invest your money in other things. Perhaps you might invest in buying stuff for your kids or you help your dad or your mum out, you might give money away to charity or you might just start up a new business or some other new project, watching people become good at what they do. The energy you can get every day when you turn up in this start-up, trying to get through the hoops, that's the buzz. They're the experiences you get out of your life if you invest your money in business. And that experience is ongoing. Every single day is a new experience. So, for me, my dream garage is actually having a start-up garage, every day's a new experience. That's perfect.

Always be looking at the next step

There's no point in running a delicatessen and just going to the delicatessen every day and doing the same thing over and over again. You may earn some money, which of course is fine, but if you are running a successful business, you've got to start thinking, *What now? Okay, should I be looking at buying the delicatessen down the road that's going broke and closing down, so everyone just comes to my shop? Or should I be trying to merge my delicatessen with somebody else so that, between the two of us, we control everything around this neighbourhood?*

What should I be doing next? Make a positive decision about that, to make it happen. Hold yourself accountable or get someone to hold you accountable.

'Partners are important in business.'

If I'd run Wizard on my own, which I could have, with no partners, I would never have grown it as fast. It might have reached the same point, but I would never have been able to do anything else. And when you can't do anything else, your brain gets stultified because you need the process of bouncing things off other people, off partners.

> 'In business, especially if you're in a start-up,
> think about who your partner is or might be.'

In my case, I didn't have a marketing platform like the Packers had, so they ran all that for me. I didn't have to think about that. But Kerry Packer made me think bigger.

Don't think, *I'm not going to share my business with anyone. I want to own the whole thing myself because I don't want to be accountable to anybody.* If you think that way, then don't expect your business to grow at the same speed as mine will, because I will get greater market share than you will. Sure, you might make more money, more of the total. You might get 100 per cent of the total, and I might only get 50 per cent of the total, but my total will be three or four times bigger than yours pretty quickly.

As a start-up you should always be thinking about who you need to bring to the table to execute your business plan. There're five parts to stick to: marketing, IT, infrastructure, operations and roll-out, and product manufacturing. And ask yourself, 'What am I good at?

And what do I need? Who's the person I need to get to be good at the other things? And do they want to be in partnership with me? Do they want to be my business partner?' Always think of these things.

That's what I did with Kerry Packer, ABN AMRO and Deutsche Bank. ABN AMRO and Deutsche Bank brought liquidity to the business. I needed to tell people what we sold. Kerry brought marketing platforms for the business, that was the Channel 9 platform. I needed to have the ability to supply the money in that market, otherwise I got nothing.

I don't care how good your brand is if you can't supply in that business you need to think about these things.

Soft skills

There's an emotional skill set in business as opposed to the hard skills. This isn't a book about hard skills. People can go and get a book or go online to learn how to advertise on Google and how to get the Search Engine Optimisation (SEO) right.

There is a shitload of stuff out there to learn hard skills but there's very little out there about soft skills. Remember how Kerry Packer asked me three questions? They're all soft skills, three soft-skill questions. Not one person in that due diligence process, which would have cost them a million bucks to do, asked me those questions at all. All that they were asking about were the hard skills like modelling and liquidity.

I was attracted to the people with hard skills post-GFC. What took me a long time to work out was that I needed the soft skills too, which actually are difficult skills to develop.

I needed to look for people with soft skills rather than being overly impressed by people with hard skills. People who had come from banks knew about financial planning and knew to do a financial plan. Those people were everywhere. It's the soft-skilled people who can also do the hard skills, they're the bunch you've got to find.

What are the soft skills you need to find?

Soft skills are things like accountability and understanding your business purpose, which all of a sudden has become a big deal. The ability to intellectually pivot. I don't mean pivoting in the sense that everyone talks about normally, but intellectually pivot. Be open-minded. When is the right time to change your business concept and what is the right concept? What is a subtle change? What are the subtle changes you can make?

Then, all of a sudden, you've got a totally different product from where you were. Don't get too caught up in what you think. You can't sit down to legislate and prescribe what something is going to look like in three or four years' time. And if you do know and you stick to that plan, that's not going to work because too many people are legislative about the way it's going to happen in their planning. Plan, yeah, but don't legislate. Prescribe now but don't expect that prescription to stay the way it is. It could change tomorrow, more so in this era than ever. You have to be nimble, adaptable and prepared for change even when you don't know what that change will be.

'One thing that is a definite at the moment is change.'

And it's faster. People talk about Moore's Law – that the technology built today will be obsolete in two years' time. I think in terms of change generally in the business cycle there's a new law. Let's call it Bouris's Law:

'Things change at a faster rate now and are changing at a faster rate every month than I've ever seen.'

In the Wizard days, nothing really changed that much for a ten-year period but now since the GFC and with the ongoing impact of COVID-19 everything is changing far more rapidly.

•

GE was the world's largest company at the time I sold to them, in terms of market capitalisation and certainly in terms of influence. Probably revenues and profits too, to some extent, but always depending on what was happening with Exxon: Exxon and GE swapped places depending on the price of oil.

It was a very different environment for me to be the chair of Wizard in Australia and New Zealand under GE's ownership. I coasted along for a couple of years. One year actually, one and a half years, and then I decided to put to GE that me and Packer, James Packer not Kerry, would coinvest with GE into setting up Wizard in emerging markets around the world.

Our first market was India, so it was a 60–40 deal with GE. We were 40 per cent, they were 60 per cent. GE, myself and James formed a global board of which I was the chair and we met with the US-based GE directors two or three times a year. I went to India every five weeks for five days to set up the business, which was a mission because India has to be by far the greatest bureaucracy in the world; one of the things the English bequeathed to India.

The English left India but they left behind the red tape of bureaucracy and the Indians completely adopted it and made it their own. It made sense in a country of such a vast population. People take the piss out of bureaucracies but the other side of the coin is that there's a job for everyone in India. You might only be getting a dollar an hour, but you've still got a job, so India was a massive eye-opener for me.

It was confronting at the beginning, seeing the poverty. I was out there giving US$100 bills out the window of my car. I was being picked up by my driver who still WhatsApps me every single day, every day, with the saying of the day. Veejay, his name is. He used to pick me up at the airport with a bunch of flowers and I'd say, 'Give them to your wife.'

'No, no, Mr Mark, they're for you.'

The poverty was confronting, and the difference between the very poor and everybody else was stark. The hotel I stayed at was unbelievable. The Trident Hotel it was called, just outside of New Delhi, very close to a town called Gurgaon. It was only twenty k's out of Delhi, but it used to take about two and a half hours to drive there because of the traffic, so Veejay and I got to know each other very well.

The hotel was raised off the ground with a big wall around it. Inside, it was absolute luxury. Just ridiculous luxury. Luxurious grounds and parks and lush greenery –

summer, winter it didn't make any difference. And outside the wall was abject poverty. Literally, outside the wall, people were living in shanties, tin sheds, just filth and rubbish.

The frenetic pace of India taught me a lot. India thrives on absolute freneticism. But yet, at the same time, you've got this crazy bureaucracy where you can't get anything approved. We were applying for an official licence to be what's called a non-bank, a non-bank but a financial institution, a BFI. It took us a couple of years to get it and then we built fifty-five Wizard branches throughout India. We became the fourth-largest lender in the state of Uttar Pradesh, the most populous state in India. In a pretty short period we had quite a lot of staff. Our objective was to go from India to Russia, then to Mexico and Brazil; GE had representation in all those places.

GE wanted me to take the Wizard idea to these BRICS countries – BRICS being the association of five emerging national economies: Brazil, Russia, India, China and South Africa – but then the GFC hit and GE basically pulled out of financial services everywhere.

At one stage I was going to move to the UK and live there, only because it would've been easier for me to get to Australia and to New Zealand and to India from London than it would've been from anywhere else. There was a flight that used to go from London to Delhi overnight. Whereas from Sydney to Delhi was a mission, it was seventeen hours. You had to fly from Sydney to Singapore then Singapore to Delhi.

It was an interesting building project for me. Building the business, building the distribution, telling the story as we became quite a large non-bank lender in India. We used the General Electric balance sheet to lend our own money, or to lend their money, so we weren't lending money on behalf of anybody else. We weren't a broker; we were lending GE money. GE had been in India I think for 100 years, so they were a big balance sheet in India and were involved in all sorts of things, like power stations.

The GFC killed it all and we sold out of that for nothing. No money. Zero. GE just pulled up stumps and without the balance sheet we couldn't go anywhere. We needed their balance sheet to fund the loans, so GE bought us out for nothing. It was around that time that GE released me from all my constraints and restraints. That was the end of my relationship with them.

Then I set up Yellow Brick Road. It was born in the middle of the GFC. It was listed in 2010 and I'm still running it. I'm still the largest individual shareholder, I'm still the chairman. It's a pretty big business, a much bigger business than Wizard ever was. And I am proud of that. That shows my resilience and ability to pivot.

What to do in the worst years

My two worst years were 2009 and 2019. In 2009, the GFC bit and that was the year that GE decided that they had to get out of financial services. My whole global initiative of Wizard being everywhere around the world, in partnership with GE, was killed off overnight. I got through it.

Then, in 2019, we had the Hayne Royal Commission. Yellow Brick Road are a listed public company. We have to report our half-yearly accounts, audited accounts which at that time had to be lodged by the end of February 2019 for the year that ended on 31 December 2018. At the beginning of February 2019, the Honourable Justice Hayne came out with his recommendations.

I had organically built Yellow Brick Road but we had bought a number of brokerages – one called Vow and another one called RESI – and they were in our balance sheet. I'd paid $35 million for them. They were in my balance sheet for that amount. When Justice Hayne dropped his bombshell about killing all the brokerage industry, or made his recommendations, our auditors, and us to some extent, right at the last minute, started thinking, *Well, we've got to write off $35 million worth of assets.* So we did. I reported a $35 million loss. Like, that's pretty crazy.

I reported that loss on about 3 or 4 March for the 31 December period, and I sat down and thought, *Wow, that's nine years of this and that's where I am, with the stroke of a pen. That's my business. But all the other 70,000 brokerages would have also had to write off the value of their business too.* I had to take the write-off because I'm a listed public company. I had obligations to disclose things.

I announced that, and realised that the changes meant I had to restructure my business. So, I immediately started to do that. I announced, when I put those numbers out, that I'd be selling my wealth business, because I had a wealth advice business. The Hayne Royal Commission made it impossible for me to deliver wealth advice, and for anyone else to deliver wealth advice. My belief still is that every Australian deserves good quality financial advice. My whole purpose with Yellow Brick Road was not only to do mortgages but to ensure people could access that good quality financial advice from a trusted source, whether you're James Packer or James Smith, who lives in Ashfield and is working as a shelf-packer at Woolworths. I was trying to democratise advice, but the Royal Commission obligations that came out were so onerous that the cost of delivering advice to James Smith was so expensive that I could never make money out of it. I would lose money, so I knew I could no longer be in this business.

I said I would sell. I was going to restructure my whole business and concentrate on mortgages and introduce my own mortgage product. To that date, we were selling the loans of other entities and banks. We were just repackaging them and selling for them. It was a pretty good business, a big business in terms of volume, but I said, 'No, I'm going to build up my own product.'

By 30 June I sold one of my wealth arms. I've only recently completed the sale of that wealth arm, in terms of money. By the beginning of 2020, I had restructured my business and completely cut the guts out of my costs. I still work incredibly long hours because a lot of the people I had to let go were top level management who were expensive. I now have to do all that work. I've also entered into a partnership with one of the world's largest hedge funds. That took two years to put together. We've just released our joint product. It's our own mortgage; we fund it. It's not a product where we sell to banks or mortgage brokers. We sell our own product. We set our own price. We set our own parameters, subject to market conditions, but we set it all. We're in control.

'I no longer want to be put into the control of anybody else.'

Everything I'd been building got smashed in the recommendations from the banking royal commission. It was going to pull apart what I'd been working on for ten years at Yellow Brick Road, but also during my whole life working at Wizard, too. Part of me was of course thinking, *How can they?* I never got called in. They never discussed it with me. I'm considered an expert in this industry. Nobody asked me about it. I never had one discussion with anybody there. Nobody.

No one would have known how I was feeling. I didn't tell anybody. I wanted to fight back. The problem was the government were in favour of what we were saying. The Turnbull government at the time was in favour.

Then it became the Morrison government and an election was called. So, what I was being confronted with in 2019 was, is Labor going to win and what's their position? And, generally speaking, the opposition takes the opposite approach from the government. I don't have any insights into Labor. I don't have the connections in Labor. I'm more well connected with the Liberal Party. I spent a lot of my own money helping the Liberals' campaign. I sent out 350,000 robocalls, which I paid for, to people saying, 'Be careful when you come to thinking about your vote. Be careful who you vote for.'

I got criticised roundly for it, people were saying, 'Mark Bouris is the human face of the Liberal Party.' That was a risk I was prepared to take. I believed in it. I needed the government to get back in because they agreed with me about saving the mortgage industry. Of course I was going to back my business and that meant backing them.

This is politics, I guess. Both sides just destroy everybody who's against them. That's the process. Nothing's changed from ancient times to today. Kings and queens, and all the people who surround them, all the politicians who surround them, will attack people when they think they're a one-off. And I was a one-off. I was just having my say. I was being rebellious. I was made out to be a heretic, which is why I want to build an army, because then you're not a heretic. Then you're something. Someone. Or your beliefs have to be considered. Your views, which are the views of others as well, are to be respected.

Back in my Wizard and early Yellow Brick Road days, I was running a one-man band. I don't want to have to do that again.

Now what I'm trying to do is build something that unites me with others.

I want you to know this because it's a good example of how small business can get crushed by something that's not part of your business, or someone who doesn't do what you do.

There're over 2 million small business owners in Australia. They're all independent people. They don't have one voice at the moment.

Well, I want to do something about that. I want to build an army. I will tell you more soon.

FIVE STEPS YOU NEED TO KNOW IF YOU ARE SERIOUS ABOUT BUILDING A BUSINESS

1. Know what you want to do and what you are prepared to sacrifice for it. The truth is something always has to give.
2. Pick your partner or team wisely – look for people with strengths that will complement your own.
3. There is more to business than spreadsheets and numbers. You need the skills to deal with all sorts of people.
4. Don't do what is popular, do what is right for you and your business.
5. Know when it is time to find a new project and don't stay too long at the party.

Who's In Your Corner?

The late Rene Rivkin was a client of the law firm I was at. One day Rene went to David Baffsky, the senior partner, and said, 'I'd like to buy Mark. I'd like to pay you the transfer fee for Mark to come and work for me.' I was a young man at the time and it was very flattering.

David told me about the conversation. I can't remember what the figure was Rene said he'd pay me, it was a lot of money though, much more than what I was earning. I think he guaranteed me a million dollars over a three-year period. I was only in my late twenties so it was ridiculous money. He was going to pay David money too, because David would lose earnings due to me leaving. I asked, 'What do I do?' and David said, 'The only advice I can give you is, whatever happens, you've got to look after your own corner because no one else will.'

He was basically saying, 'Don't think you've got to stay here at the law firm because you've got to be nice to me, but don't think you've got to take up Rene's offer because he's nice to you. Just remember you're going to be out there on your own.'

'Look after your own corner, no one else will.'

I like boxing and I also know that, in business, like boxing, the moment you walk into that ring, you're on your own. It doesn't matter who's around you – when you're in the ring you're on your own. It's one of the reasons I fight every year. People think I fight because I want to represent the New South Wales Police and raise money. That's true, I do, but that's not my only purpose.

The second reason I fight is to get fit. It takes three months to build up to a fight period – three months. You lose weight, you get fit, you don't drink, you don't eat shit. It's good for your body and that's important.

But, again, that's not the main reason I do it. The primary reason I do it is because I like to remind myself what it's like to be in the ring on your own. No one's going to help you and it doesn't matter how hard you prepare for it or what you do, you're going to be confronted with things you didn't expect. You have to tough it out, same as business, same as right now.

It's nerve-racking. It doesn't matter what anybody says, it doesn't matter how hard you train, how much experience you have – the adrenaline rush and the nervousness you get before you jump in the ring on the night is confronting. For me, it's the same every year. I'm sixty-four and I've been fighting forever. It happens the day of the fight mostly, although sometimes in the week before and the build-up to that night. You walk in there and you know that bloke is going to try and beat the shit out of you. You get brought to this point of realisation: this is it. You want to stop yourself from getting hurt. I'm not scared of it, I don't have fear, but it's just the realisation of the edginess of it. I remind myself of that feeling all the time and that's what it's like in business.

Lots of people carry on about it but not many actually step in the ring. Just like running a business. I know because I have actually stepped in the ring many times, and I know what that feeling's like. It's intense. No one else can help you. You can sit down at the break, they can put some water on your head, and they can say, 'Slip', or 'Duck', or 'Step to his right', or whatever. That's all fucking bullshit. It's not something you can necessarily do. You and I both know how that feels when you're running your own business.

> 'It's all about how well you prepare before
> you get there.'

Even though you can't prepare for that specific moment in the ring, the fact that you have done the work gives you the best shot to come out a winner. Knowing you are fit, knowing you can go the distance because of the work you have put in. And then that moment comes. That's when you're on your own. When you're on your own with your own thoughts, in your own world. That's what boxing's all about. That's what running a business is all about. It's all about being able to deal with your thoughts. Sometimes you've got to stand in the corner and cop the punches, other times you've got to move out of the way even though you don't think you can, sometimes you've got to throw punches back and, to me, it's a metaphor for life. You have to jump in the ring and fight.

I probably shouldn't be boxing at my age, but it reminds me what it's like to survive as a person, whether it's in a team or on your own.

'The closest metaphor to running a business I
know is to be physically in the ring, up against
someone. In my case they are usually much
younger and bigger. Sometimes you've got to
fight a bigger opponent, sometimes in business
you're taking on a bigger business.'

Let's continue the parallels. I enjoy the preparation period, I enjoy the objective and purpose and goals that I have, it gives me something to work towards.

For me it's a proper battle. It's a strategic battle too. You've got to think about what you're doing. You need to know what your opponent's strengths and weaknesses are. You've got to go in with a plan although the plan doesn't necessarily always help you when you're in the ring.

Whether you run a small or medium-sized business, if you're a sole trader or a self-employed person of some kind, then you'll probably identify with what I'm describing: the mentality and mindset of the person who decides to be their own boss, decides to strike out on their own.

'Underline the word *own*, as in "on your
fucking own, by yourself", because that's
what it is, that's what you're in for.'

When you're in the business arena it's like being in the boxing ring, because there's no one who's going to suddenly come to your aid. Someone might give you some advice, 'Look, maybe you should do this with your marketing or maybe you could change your website.' But no one's going to do it for you. They're not going to be there when the blows are landing left, right and centre. When the GST bill comes in and you can't pay, no one's going to help out. No one gives you any money, nobody. No one's going to be there at three o'clock in the morning when you're going over the latest health protocols you'll have to set up in your store when the doors open in a few hours.

If there is one thing I've learned about business, it's that only the tough survive. In a world of airy-fairy bullshit, where people wait for the universe to provide, there is one thing you need to know: the universe provides you nothing. You have to take it. So, you'd better like eating rocks and taking hits. Because this ride isn't easy.

It's why I love boxing. And, if I'm being totally honest with you, why I like taking a punch to the face every now and again. Not only does it remind me I'm alive, but it reminds me that you can't afford to leave anything in the ring or the opponent you're fighting will sense it and take you apart. Business, at least a successful one, is no different.

I know people who are great baristas, they had unbelievable training, they're good-looking in that way that baristas are, they've got the whole thing going. They want to open a coffee shop, but they fall apart because they're on their own.

If you feel as though you are doing the right thing, if you're in there for the right reasons, then you're like me. I'll go in and I'll die going down. I might be sixty-four but I'm not going to kowtow, at this point in my life, to what I don't believe in just so I can have a peaceful life. I'm just not doing it. That's not my nature.

I could ride off into the sunset, but I'm not going to. This is what I've been put here to do. This is my purpose. I'm here to represent. I'm here to protect. I'm here to make it better or make it as good as it can be and I'm not going to allow people, the system, to take away from hardworking people like my dad, my uncles, my friends, my contemporaries, my colleagues, you. I'm just not going to let the system take it away from them or you.

Fuck that! As much as we all know as a business owner it is on your head, that you have to do the hard work and you're the one making things happen, there are things you can do to help yourself. I hope that this book and my mentoring program, podcasts and newspaper columns can guide you to answer the questions you need to ask yourself to succeed. Don't ever be afraid of giving a wrong answer, just ensure you have an answer that works for you. This country was built on hard work, ambition, innovation, early risers, hustlers and big thinkers, so be one of them!

A Call to Action

I'm glad you've read the book, glad you bought it, I really appreciate it, I hope you got something out of it.

Back at the start of the book I talked about building a warrior army of small business owners. I want to return to that idea now. What I'm trying to do is to take the temperature of the business community at this very pivotal time to find out if I'm the only person thinking the way I do about the precarious nature of our business landscape, or are there 20,000 people thinking this way? Maybe I am the only person thinking this?

If you're in business and you survived 2020, if you were still standing at the end of the year, then well done. We all know it's been a tough year, no matter what you do, no matter what your trade. Business owners are hardened warriors, hardened people, hardened through good and bad experiences, the best warriors you're ever going to want, every time. Anyone right now with an ABN, anyone who is a contractor or is self-employed, anyone who is a sole trader or a consultant, is anyone talking to you, and looking after you? I don't think there is.

All you get every now and then is a politician saying, 'We really want to help small business. You're the heartbeat of the country.' Okay, well, what the fuck are you doing then? Don't talk spin to us. Do something.

I'm fed up with waiting for the government to act. I don't think patience is in my DNA. We need governments to govern for us, not for them, not for what they think. Govern for us. Because we're the ones who vote for them. As soon as we start talking votes that's when governments pay attention. So let's get their attention! Let's form a society. If we get enough people and enough businesses to join together, the government will stop and listen. Who am I talking about? Anyone who's not getting their super, holiday pay or sick pay paid by someone else.

'Anyone who's not getting a weekly or monthly wage dropped into their bank account, I'm talking to you.'

If we can find out how many people feel the government isn't considering them we'll know if we have the numbers to change that. A social experiment. If my hunch is correct and Australians do care about our business community, then I'll do something about it. You've got my commitment on that. You won't die wondering and nor will I, because I'll make it my business to take it somewhere and I won't stop. I will hammer them. I will just keep going at 'em, going at 'em, going at 'em.

People keep asking, 'Who's going to stand up?' Well, fuck it, I'll stand up. If I cop the rough end of the pineapple because I do, that's bad luck for me. It won't stop me.

'The solution is, to build an army.'

If we went back 10,000 years and we were looking to stand up for ourselves against those in power making decisions that were for them not the majority, I would be on my horse, my sturdy steed, and I'd be visiting where all the small business owners are. I'd be trying to garner their support so I could turn up to parliament with 20,000 warriors. That's how I would build an army. In *Braveheart*, William Wallace did exactly this, he brought all these Scottish warriors into one place and then he confronted the English. It's exactly the same deal (without the horse).

Nothing's changed, just the technology. So, then the question becomes, 'How should I do this today, what technology should I use to build this small business army?' I think I know what will work. I will build a platform. It will be called the Business Warriors. I will put information up on my mentoring website, mentored.com.au

I need to ask you to sign up and tell me what your concerns are so we (a) know what our list of demands are; (b) put together a petition; and (c) petition the government and the upper end of town with our log of claims: the banks, the government, insurance companies and landlords.

Over a period of three or four months, I'll get the collective thoughts curated, nothing will be left out, no voice or thought will be too insignificant. What do 75 per cent of people want, what do 65 per cent want, what do 25 per cent want, right through to 1 per cent. That's our log of claims, most important through to least important. I'll feed it back to everybody and let everybody know what the outcomes are. Then, I'll take it forward. To all intents and purposes, this army is us forming a society of small businesses. A society that brings together all self-employed, all sole-traders and all small business owners into one place to fight for what we need to strengthen our businesses and secure our futures.

What I haven't done, is I haven't actually asked anyone to sign up to anything. Until now. Now I'm asking you to sign up to be battle-ready, because we need to develop our log of claims and you need to communicate what you think. What are the things that need to be addressed. I don't care what you say, just say it. Tell me what you think.

To get the attention we're after, the more of us there are, the better, so we can become a real lobby group, the Business Warriors. Then I will take it to the government.

We need numbers. It's not just my say-so. I might have good relationships with the politicians and they might take me seriously, but they're not going to move unless they know they're going to lose votes or they're going to have a war. They don't want that. Nobody wants that. To get someone to the table, they need to know they are either going to gain something or lose something. We need to make the government realise they better pay attention.

It could be, that Australians are totally apathetic. That's quite possible. It could be that this is just my own style of thinking, but that's okay. This is a good way of finding out if others feel the same and want to make a difference.

I'm prepared to stand behind what I believe. I'm prepared to create this platform. I'm prepared to see if

Australian small business owners are apathetic or not. This is a social experiment for me, so the result will inform me and others. I'm not invested in the outcome per se, but I have a belief about what I think the outcome will be, but if it doesn't turn out the way I think, so be it. No one loses here. If it doesn't work, it doesn't work.

People have been asking me, 'Are you going to become a politician?' No, I'm not, but I want to use the influence I have to do what I can for the people I believe in. And the people I believe in are small business owners. People today use their influence to sway consumers, I want to use my influence to create positive change. But I can't do that unless I know people are supporting what I'm saying. I think this is relevant. I'm happy to start the conversation, but you've got to tell me if the conversation is worth having. Please leave comments on the website and I will read them all.

I would also like to organise some events, so stay tuned for updates on the website.

If you've read this book and connected to it and want to join this platform, share it with somebody else. I'm not looking for more sales so put it on your Instagram – not the book – the idea of the small business army and its objectives. Go to your social media platforms – Instagram, Facebook, LinkedIn – and put the ideas and the link to the platform out there. We can use our collective power to get others to share the conversation and get things started.

It was Margaret Mead, the American author, speaker and cultural anthropologist who said, 'Never doubt that a small group of thoughtful, committed citizens can change the world; indeed, it's the only thing that ever has.'

Our small group of committed people, our army, starts right here. This is the call to action.

Join me.

Mark Bouris

Find out more information about Mark Bouris,
his Mentored platform and podcast at:

markbouris.com.au
mentored.com.au

* * *

For speaking and commercial enquiries for
Mark Bouris contact:

thefordhamcompany.com.au

hachette
AUSTRALIA

If you would like to find out more about
Hachette Australia, our authors, upcoming events
and new releases you can visit our website
or our social media channels:

hachette.com.au
HachetteAustralia
HachetteAus